ILLINOIS TRIVIA

ILLINOIS TRIVIA

Compiled by Robert Cromie

RUTLEDGE HILL PRESS
Nashville, Tennessee

Published by Rutledge Hill Press, Inc.
513 Third Avenue South
Nashville, Tennessee 37210

Typography by D&T/Bailey Typesetters, Nashville, Tennessee

Library of Congress Cataloging-in-Publication Data

Cromie, Robert 1909–
    Illinois trivia / Robert Cromie.
        p.   cm.
    ISBN 1-55853-162-9
    1. Illinois—Miscellanea.   2. Questions and answers.   I. Title.
F541.5.C761992
977.3′0076—dc20   92-9312
                                                                        CIP

Printed in the United States of America
2 3 4 5 6 7—97 96 95 94 93

PREFACE

All it takes to fashion a book of trivia is a collection of more or less interesting tidbits of information; though it helps if one knows where to look. A major source of this particular gathering was the "Chicago History" booklet of the Chicago Historical Society, which included in most issues a listing of 50-year-old newspaper headlines. Also valuable were such annual publications as *The Guinness Book of Records, The Information Please Almanac, The World Almanac;* a volume listing the state's historical markers; numerous Illinois histories; the Chicago newspapers (especially the columnists); and—the list is incomplete—a well-worn copy of *The Baseball Encyclopedia,* picked up at a library sale for twenty-five cents. Add such kindly folk as George Cohen and Kenan Heise of the *Tribune;* Irene McMahon, who took time between travel articles to inform me of trivial things; and my own freakish memory for the flotsam and jetsam of existence.

I shall be unhappy to be apprised of any errors or serious omissions, but am prepared to find someone to blame such trivia on. Meanwhile, happy reading.

For Alice, *con amore*

TABLE OF CONTENTS

GEOGRAPHY

C H A P T E R   O N E

Q. When did Illinois become the twenty-first state?

A. December 3, 1818.

———◆———

Q. What Indian word means skunk cabbage, wild onion, garlic, great, or a line of Indian chiefs?

A. *Che-cau-gou.*

———◆———

Q. What is now on the site of the O'Leary cottage?

A. The Chicago Fire Academy.

———◆———

Q. Why was Canton, Illinois, so named?

A. Because its founder believed it and Canton, China, were antipodal.

———◆———

Q. Why is there a statue of Elijah Lovejoy in Alton?

A. He was murdered there in 1837 by a mob for his anti-slavery views.

Q. What body of water did the French call *Lac des Illinois?*

A. Lake Michigan.

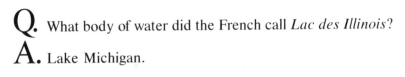

Q. Where is the village in which Abraham Lincoln lived from 1831-1837?

A. Now restored, it is in New Salem Park near Springfield.

Q. Where was the first Illinois zoning ordinance passed?

A. Evanston, in 1921.

Q. How much was in the municipal treasury when Chicago became a city in 1837?

A. $1,193.

Q. How did Aledo get its name in 1851?

A. Letters were drawn out of a hat and the first pronounce-able set spelled A-L-E-D-O.

Q. Where was Lincoln nominated for the presidency in 1860?

A. The newly erected Wigwam in Chicago.

Q. Why was the Thirty-third Regiment of the Illinois Volunteers in the Civil War called the "Brains Regiment"?

A. It contained many volunteers from Illinois State University, Normal.

Q. Delegates to the Republican convention in Chicago in 1860 were irked by what "exorbitant" charge for bed and board?

A. $1.50 to $2.50 per day.

———◆———

Q. Who were the first white settlers in what is now southern Illinois?

A. The French, circa 1700.

———◆———

Q. Illinois contains how many square miles?

A. 56,400.

———◆———

Q. What was the first river in the world to be altered to flow "backward," away from its natural mouth?

A. Chicago River, in 1900 made to flow westward from Lake Michigan, to carry away sewage and become part of a canal system.

———◆———

Q. What city has two parks named Scovill?

A. Decatur.

———◆———

Q. What is the northwesternmost town in Illinois?

A. East Dubuque.

———◆———

Q. The steel-arch structure over the Mississippi River connecting St. Louis, Missouri, and East St. Louis, Illinois, was named for what engineer and inventor who during the Civil War built the first gunboats armored with iron plates?

A. James Buchanan Eads.

Q. At 1,235 feet, what is the highest point in Illinois?

A. Charles Mound.

———◆———

Q. What are the three nicknames for Illinois?

A. Inland Empire, Land of Lincoln, and Prairie State.

———◆———

Q. With 110 stories, the Sears Tower in Chicago is the world's tallest building at how many feet?

A. 1,454.

———◆———

Q. What manufacturing and trading center in the great dairy region of northern Illinois lies on the Fox River about thirty-eight miles northwest of Chicago?

A. Elgin.

———◆———

Q. What is the Illinois state motto?

A. State Sovereignty—National Union.

———◆———

Q. What percentage of Illinois residents live in metropolitan areas?

A. More than 80 percent.

———◆———

Q. What rank among the states is Illinois in corn production?

A. Second only to Iowa.

Q. Prehistoric Indians called Mound Builders left evidence of their once-flourishing Mississippian civilization, the center of an enormous trade empire distinguished by social and political activity, at what place in Illinois?

A. Cahokia Mounds State Historic Site, between Cahokia and East St. Louis.

Q. What is the origin of the name *Illinois?*

A. It is French for *Illini*, an Algonquin word meaning "men" or "warriors."

Q. The Illinois River starts at the meeting of what two rivers?

A. Kankakee and Des Plaines.

Q. Where is the geographic center of Illinois?

A. Logan, twenty-eight miles northeast of Springfield.

Q. When it was founded in 1816, what was the name given to present-day East St. Louis?

A. Illinoistown.

Q. What is the average length of the state?

A. 390 miles.

Q. For whom was O'Hare International Airport named?

A. Lt. Comdr. Edward ("Butch") O'Hare, a pilot killed at the battle of Midway.

Q. What was Chicago's population when the River and Harbor Convention drew more than 20,000 visitors to the city in July 1847?

A. About 16,000.

———◆———

Q. Where was the home of Mormon leader Joseph Smith?

A. Nauvoo.

———◆———

Q. Where does Illinois rank in the nation in export of agricultural products?

A. First.

———◆———

Q. Why is Galena a favorite tourist mecca?

A. Because of sixty antique shops and forty bed-and-breakfast establishments.

———◆———

Q. The largest of the Hyatt chain's 159 hotels and resorts, the Hyatt Regency in Chicago, contains how many guest rooms?

A. 2,033.

———◆———

Q. What U.S. president was born in Tampico?

A. Ronald Reagan, who grew up in nearby Dixon.

———◆———

Q. Erected in 1832, what was Chicago's first public building?

A. A pen for loose livestock.

Q. Where was noted American historian Allan Nevins born?

A. Camp Point, on an old Indian trail.

———◆———

Q. What city banned the sale of liquor from 1853 to 1971?

A. Evanston.

———◆———

Q. What city is known as the Soy Bean Capital of the World?

A. Decatur.

———◆———

Q. What occupies the twenty-eight-room former home of Charles Gates Dawes?

A. The Evanston Historical Society.

———◆———

Q. For whom was Menard County named?

A. Pierre Menard, first lieutenant governor of Illinois.

———◆———

Q. How many square miles of water are in Illinois?

A. 652.

———◆———

Q. Why is baggage for O'Hare International Airport marked ORD?

A. The field's original name was Orchard.

Q. Where was Wild Bill Hickok born?

A. Troy Grove, LaSalle County.

———◆———

Q. Where in Chicago is the statue of Abraham Lincoln by Augustus Saint-Gaudens?

A. Grant Park.

———◆———

Q. Illinois's largest artificial lake, Crab Orchard Lake near Carbondale, covers how many acres?

A. 7,000.

———◆———

Q. Where in Chicago is Ulysses S. Grant's statue?

A. Lincoln Park.

———◆———

Q. Who was the first permanent settler of Chicago?

A. Jean Baptiste Pointe du Sable, a well-educated black man.

———◆———

Q. The 187 public use areas in Illinois comprise how many acres?

A. 275,000.

———◆———

Q. Reputedly the world's tallest man at eight feet, eleven inches, Robert Pershing Wadlow was born in what city?

A. Alton (on February 22, 1918).

Q. Where is the only temple in North America for the universal religion of Bahai?

A. Wilmette.

———◆———

Q. What was the Indian name of Lake Peoria?

A. *Pimiteoui*, meaning "fat lake."

———◆———

Q. When did Abraham Lincoln become an Illinoisan?

A. Born in Kentucky, later a resident of Indiana, he moved to Illinois in 1830.

———◆———

Q. What ordinances did the Chicago city council pass in 1898 governing buildings?

A. None over 130 feet tall and fire escapes on any over four stories.

———◆———

Q. How many acres of forested land are in Illinois?

A. 3,810,400.

———◆———

Q. Where was Dexter Mathews, former director of Consumers Union and a University of Chicago graduate, born?

A. Springfield.

———◆———

Q. Why did the Chicago Motor Club in 1909 install road signs between Chicago and Milwaukee, Wisconsin, except for the last fifteen miles?

A. That section was impassable.

Q. Where did Wabash County get its name?

A. It comes from an Indian word meaning "white water."

———◆———

Q. What indicated that Chicago had become the world's convention center?

A. Fourteen national conventions in Chicago in August 1907, with twenty set for September.

———◆———

Q. What was the original name of Lake Bluff?

A. Rockland.

———◆———

Q. What Evanston pioneer has two streets named for him?

A. Orrington Lunt.

———◆———

Q. Why was the Mississippi River between Cairo and St. Louis once known to steamboat men as the "Graveyard"?

A. More than 300 boats had been wrecked in that sector by 1867.

———◆———

Q. By what action during the Revolution did the Illinois region become a county of Virginia?

A. George Rogers Clark of Virginia captured Kaskaskia and Cahokia from the English in 1778.

———◆———

Q. How much land, which later became a large portion of Chicago, did Robert A. Kinzie buy in 1831?

A. 102 acres for a total of $127.68.

Q. What marks the western terminus of the Cumberland or National Road, which covers 591 miles from Cumberland, Maryland, to Illinois?

A. The Madonna of the Trail statue in Vandalia.

———◆———

Q. For whom was Carroll County named?

A. Charles Carroll, the last surviving signer of the Declaration of Independence.

———◆———

Q. How many Chicagoans made reservations for the inauguration of President McKinley?

A. More than 2,500.

———◆———

Q. How long did it take a Lake Shore and Michigan Southern train to make its record-breaking run between Chicago and Buffalo on October 24, 1895?

A. Seven hours, fifty minutes, twenty seconds.

———◆———

Q. What was the lowest rent for an eighteen-room apartment in a new building under construction in 1914 on Michigan Avenue in Chicago?

A. $8,400 yearly.

———◆———

Q. How much did Chicago's Auditorium hotel, theater, and office building bring at a tax sale in 1911?

A. The property, valued at $4,000,000, went for $46,680.

———◆———

Q. When were three-inch-high house numbers required for residences in Chicago?

A. September 1, 1909.

Q. According to *Forbes* magazine's 1991 list of the 400 richest Americans, what two Chicago residents tied for wealthiest in the state?

A. Jay Arthur Pritzker and Robert Alan Pritzker, at $2.25 billion.

———◆———

Q. How many Chicagoans made steamer reservations to attend the coronation of King George V on June 22, 1911?

A. Five thousand.

———◆———

Q. Whose "Plan for Chicago" anticipated by thirty years the need for transportation, parks, and residential development on a metropolitan scale?

A. Architect Daniel Hudson Burnham.

———◆———

Q. What had Chicagoan Lambert Tree done two days before dying in New York in October 1910, at the age of seventy-eight?

A. Made his 122d Atlantic crossing.

———◆———

Q. What did the Chicago city council abolish in public places on May 8, 1911?

A. The common drinking cup.

———◆———

Q. What gift from King Louis XV of France to the Church of the Immaculate Conception near Kaskaskia Island is said to have been the first west of the Appalachians?

A. A church bell.

———◆———

Q. What was the city of Galena once famous for?

A. Producing 85 percent of the nation's lead.

Q. How many slaves are believed to have escaped by way of the Underground Railroad routes passing through Illinois?

A. About 75,000.

------◆------

Q. What bequest did "Black George," a former slave, leave when he died in Otterville in 1864?

A. $1,500 for a monument to his former owner, Dr. Silas Hamilton, who freed thirty-eight slaves during his lifetime.

------◆------

Q. Why is the "Long Nine Museum" in Athens of historic interest?

A. Because in 1837 citizens gave a banquet there for Lincoln and eight other legislators from Sangamon County.

------◆------

Q. Which of Lincoln's teachers is buried in Farmers Point cemetery near New Salem?

A. Mentor Graham, who taught Lincoln in 1833.

------◆------

Q. What Illinois community is said to have been the first planned industrial town in the nation?

A. The model town of Pullman, where employees of George Pullman's sleeping-car factory were housed—at rents much higher than Chicago's.

------◆------

Q. Founded in 1847 as Rockford Female Seminary, then becoming Rockford College in 1892, the institution first admitted male students in what year?

A. 1955.

------◆------

Q. How many members of the Catholic Total Abstinence Union of America met in convention at Chicago's Auditorium in August 1909?

A. Five thousand.

Q. In 1907, what was the estimated cost of the world's tallest hotel, the twenty-two story LaSalle at LaSalle and Madison?

A. Six million dollars.

Q. What makes the students of Tinley Park High School a standout group?

A. They helped at a center for mentally retarded adults for the second Christmas in succession in 1991.

Q. Who heads Maryville Academy in Des Plaines, a center for sexually and emotionally abused youths, which has several satellite programs?

A. Rev. John P. Smyth, a former Notre Dame football and basketball star.

Q. When was Chicago's first public statue placed in Union Park?

A. 1907, of Carter Harrison, Sr.

Q. How many cars and visitors were at Chicago's Coliseum's Fifth Annual Auto Show in 1904?

A. Three hundred cars (costing $350 to $10,000) and 122,421 visitors.

Q. A Chicago lot on South Water Street, bought for $70 in 1832, was sold for how much in 1913?

A. $80,000.

Q. Were Chicago voters for or against building a subway in April 1914?

A. Overwhelmingly against.

Q. Part of the waterway system joining the Great Lakes with the Gulf of Mexico, the Illinois River is linked to Lake Michigan by the Des Plaines River and what canal?

A. Chicago Sanitary and Ship Canal.

———◆———

Q. What is the largest known prehistoric earthwork in the United States, covering more than fourteen acres at its base and standing one hundred feet tall?

A. Monk's Mound, at the Cahokia Mounds Site.

———◆———

Q. "Long John" Wentworth named Sandwich, Illinois, after his hometown in what state?

A. New Hampshire.

———◆———

Q. What did both Joliet and Chicago complete during 1991 as they improved their downtown areas?

A. Renovation of their run-down Union railroad stations.

———◆———

Q. What proposed high school courses did Evanston voters turn down in 1911?

A. Manual training and domestic science.

———◆———

Q. According to an announcement March 3, 1911, what would replace the Lambert Tree residence on Wabash Avenue between Ontario and Ohio streets in Chicago?

A. A new Medinah Temple.

———◆———

Q. What drew a surprising throng of 400,000 visitors during a two-week presentation at the Coliseum in May 1911?

A. The Child Welfare Exhibit, depicting the plight of Chicago's poor youngsters.

Q. In 1675, Father Jacques Marquette founded a mission at the Kaskaskia Indian village near the present site of what city?

A. Utica.

Q. At what point does the Mississippi River double in volume?

A. Cairo, where the Ohio River joins it.

Q. What halted the building of new homes in Chicago most of May 1911?

A. A brickmakers' strike.

Q. More than eighty years ago, what did a mayor's commission report about the state of the Cook County Hospital building?

A. That it was badly overcrowded with buildings out-of-date and in poor condition.

Q. In December 1904, why did E. A. S. Clarke move from his job as International Harvester general manager to head of Lackawanna Steel in New York?

A. He was offered $50,000 a year.

Q. What were the yearly earnings of Chicago members of the International Typographical Union in 1908, termed the highest of any organized trade in the United States?

A. An average of $897.

Q. What did Chicago observe on July 14, 1917, as a wartime gesture to France?

A. Bastille Day.

Q. When did regular stagecoach service between Chicago and Milwaukee begin?

A. In 1836.

———◆———

Q. What successful scheme did David D. Orr, the Cook County Clerk, devise to increase voter registration in 1991?

A. He deputized 100 seniors at seven Chicago area high schools to register friends, family, or selves.

———◆———

Q. How many bushels of wheat were loaded in one day when navigation on the Great Lakes opened March 22, 1910?

A. 4,500,000 bushels from the Chicago river elevators.

———◆———

Q. For what purpose did the city council authorize spending $65,000,000 in March 1914?

A. Building the Union Station.

———◆———

Q. Who represented Spain at the World's Columbian Exposition?

A. The Infanta Eulalia, youngest sister of King Alfonso XII.

———◆———

Q. Who donated Chicago's Buckingham Fountain in Grant Park in 1927?

A. Kate Sturges Buckingham in memory of her brother.

———◆———

Q. At what town did Abraham Lincoln and Stephen A. Douglas meet in July 1858 to plan their famous debates?

A. Bement.

Q. The abutting cities of Bloomington and Normal share the only street in the nation with what at each end?

A. A university: Illinois Wesleyan at Bloomington and Illinois State at Normal.

———◆———

Q. Where are Jane Addams's birthplace and grave?

A. Both on Mill Street in Cedarville.

———◆———

Q. At Metropolis, there is a phone booth from which a visitor can call and talk with what fictional hero?

A. Superman.

———◆———

Q. Evanston was the birthplace of what well-known political columnist?

A. Drew Pearson.

———◆———

Q. Where was the birthplace of Helen Scott Hay, a Northwestern graduate who was director of Red Cross nurses during World War I?

A. Near Lanark, Carroll County.

———◆———

Q. Who started the first detective agency in Chicago?

A. William Allan Pinkerton, a native of Scotland.

———◆———

Q. What Chicagoan became ambassador to Denmark in 1961?

A. William McCormick Blair, former administrative assistant to Adlai Stevenson.

Q. Near what town is the historic French Colonial District?

A. Prairie Du Rocher.

Q. What Catholic theologian, a native of El Paso, Illinois, hosted a popular television program in the 1950s?

A. Bishop Fulton J. Sheen, also a noted radio commentator and for years head of the philosophy department at Catholic University of America, whose TV show was called "Life Is Worth Living."

Q. In what city is the Pick Dodds Park and Heritage Park?

A. Champaign.

Q. The World War I draft brought how many Illinois residents into military service?

A. 193,338.

Q. In what town is the Log Cabin Village?

A. Kinmundy.

Q. The only town named for a president before he was elected, Lincoln was christened by what young lawyer who had prepared legal documents for the developers using watermelon juice?

A. Abraham Lincoln.

Q. What city had the largest population of Poles in the world in 1913?

A. Chicago.

Q. Why was Springfield's first airport named for Charles A. Lindbergh in 1927?

A. He helped lay it out and flew the mail into Springfield prior to his transoceanic flight.

———◆———

Q. Prior to October 1909, Loyola University of Chicago had what name?

A. Saint Ignatius College, founded in 1870.

———◆———

Q. What decision affecting Chicago's lake front did the state supreme court uphold in November 1897?

A. A suit brought by merchant Montgomery Ward to raze all buildings but the Art Institute.

———◆———

Q. When did Libertyville change its name to Independence Grove?

A. 1837, following the opening of the first post office.

———◆———

Q. The western, southern, and eastern boundaries of Illinois are formed by what three rivers?

A. Mississippi, Ohio, and Wabash, respectively.

———◆———

Q. "The finest hotel west of New York City" when it opened in 1855, the DeSoto House in Galena was remodeled and reopened in what year?

A. 1986.

———◆———

Q. For whom was Shelbyville named?

A. Revolutionary War general Isaac Shelby, later governor of Kentucky.

Q. The metropolitan area known as the Quad Cities includes Moline and Rock Island, as well as what two other cities?

A. Bettendorf and Davenport, Iowa.

———◆———

Q. Ann Rutledge, Abraham Lincoln's "lost love," is buried in a cemetery on the edge of what town?

A. Petersburg.

———◆———

Q. When two friends, George Warburton and Peter Lukins, founded the town of Petersburg in 1833, how did they name it?

A. They played cards to determine who would choose a name and Lukins won.

———◆———

Q. What were the only two public buildings to survive the Chicago fire?

A. The Old Water Tower and its pumping station.

———◆———

Q. Other than being participants in the famous "Monkey Trial" in Dayton, Tennessee, in 1925, John Thomas Scopes, the biology teacher who had broken state law by teaching evolution, and his prosecutor, William Jennings Bryan, had what in common?

A. Both were born in Salem.

———◆———

Q. For whom was the town of Gurnee named?

A. Walter Gurnee, a former mayor of Chicago.

———◆———

Q. While working there as a farmer and rail-splitter, the twenty-one-year-old Lincoln made his first political speech in what town?

A. Decatur.

Q. What city is the home of five institutions of higher learning and the headquarters of Rotary International and the Women's Christian Temperance Union?

A. Evanston.

───────◆───────

Q. What native American has two Illinois towns named for him?

A. Aptakisic, the English translation of whose name is Half Day.

───────◆───────

Q. In what Illinois county was Idaho senator William Edgar Borah born?

A. Jasper.

───────◆───────

Q. What headline attributed to a downstate newspaper humorously refers to two Illinois towns?

A. "Oblong Girl Weds Normal Boy."

───────◆───────

Q. When did Springfield become the permanent home of the Illinois State Fair?

A. 1894.

───────◆───────

Q. What was the name of Nauvoo before the Mormons settled there in 1839?

A. Commerce.

───────◆───────

Q. At the beginning of his military career, future general George S. Patton stood guard at what military base near Highwood?

A. Fort Sheridan.

Q. What town is in the northeasternmost corner of Illinois?

A. Winthrop Harbor.

———◆———

Q. For whom was Chanute Field named?

A. Octave Chanute, the French-born American engineer and aviation pioneer, who died in Chicago in 1910.

———◆———

Q. The name of Hutsonville commemorates what tragic event of 1813?

A. The massacre of the Hutson family by Indians.

———◆———

Q. What was unusual about the Charter Oak School, built near Schuline in 1873 and used for eighty years?

A. Its octagonal shape.

———◆———

Q. Where were three of the Eads ironclad vessels built for the Union during the Civil War?

A. Mound City, on the Mississippi River.

———◆———

Q. What social worker joined with Jane Addams in 1889 to found Hull House to help the foreign-born in Chicago?

A. Ellen Gates Starr.

———◆———

Q. Where did Sangamon County get its name?

A. A corruption of a native American name for "good hunting ground."

Q. Near what small town is the John Deere Home?

A. Grand Detour.

———◆———

Q. Who built the Mary Gates Dawes hotel for young women, with rooms costing ten to thirty cents nightly?

A. Chicagoan Charles G. Dawes, in tribute to his mother.

———◆———

Q. What was the site of the U.S. Navy's largest recruit training command?

A. Great Lakes Naval Training Center.

———◆———

Q. What three town names in the extreme southern tip of the state reflect the fact that the area is dubbed Little Egypt for its fertile soil and similarity to the Nile Delta?

A. Cairo, Karnak, Thebes.

———◆———

Q. Who founded Orphans of the Storm, a dog-and-cat refuge near Deerfield?

A. Irene Castle McLaughlin in 1928.

———◆———

Q. Illinois ranks first in the nation in production of what agricultural product?

A. Soybeans.

———◆———

Q. To whom does Bradley University owe its existence?

A. An eighty-one year old widow, Lydia Moss Bradley, of Peoria.

Q. How did the town of Wamac derive its name?

A. From the three counties it lies in: Washington, Marion, and Clinton.

———◆———

Q. The Illinois Waterway System comprises how many miles of navigable waterways linking the St. Lawrence Seaway with the Mississippi shipping lanes?

A. 1,110.

———◆———

Q. What county's name comes from an Indian word meaning "white potato"?

A. Macoupin.

———◆———

Q. How many miles of shoreline on Lake Michigan does Illinois have?

A. Sixty-three.

———◆———

Q. For whom was the Margaretta Post Office in Clark County named in 1840?

A. The wife of the postmaster, William B. Marrs, former state legislator.

———◆———

Q. Now a state memorial, what religious community was founded in 1846 by Swedish settlers who owned all property in common?

A. Bishop Hill, near Galva.

———◆———

Q. What woman founded Mount Carroll Seminary (later Shimer College) as a co-educational institution in 1856?

A. Frances Ann Wood.

Q. What was the first Illinois state capital?

A. Kaskaskia, 1818-1820.

———◆———

Q. Where is the Wild Bill Hickok State Memorial?

A. La Salle.

———◆———

Q. What was the vocation of Ida B. Wells, for whom the housing project on Chicago's South Side was named?

A. Newspaperwoman and social reformer.

———◆———

Q. What U.S. Air Force base near Belleville was named for the first enlisted man to die in an air accident?

A. Scott Air Force Base, named for Corp. Frank S. Scott.

———◆———

Q. Long the nation's "second city," Chicago now has what population ranking?

A. Third.

———◆———

Q. What claims to be the world's largest outlet mall?

A. Gurnee Mills, on Route 132 west of Waukegan.

———◆———

Q. What town was named for the famous commander of the *Chesapeake* during the War of 1812, whose dying command was "Don't give up the ship"?

A. Lawrenceville, for Capt. James Lawrence.

Q. Why did Area change its name to Mundelein in 1926?

A. It was changed after Cardinal George Mundelein was host for a giant Eucharistic conference at St. Mary-of-the-Lake Seminary.

Q. What did the Boston Ladies Society for the Promotion of Christian Education found in Illinois?

A. The DuQuoin Female Seminary.

Q. How did six thousand foreign-born Chicagoans observe the Fourth of July, 1916?

A. They attended a Coliseum rally and pledged allegiance to the United States.

Q. When did the town of Little Fort change its name to Waukegan, an Algonquin word meaning "fort"?

A. 1859.

Q. When did the Chicago-Waukegan segment of the road to Milwaukee open?

A. New Year's Day, 1851.

Q. What town in northern Illinois is named for a native American who twice warned the early settlers of danger from hostile tribes?

A. Shabbona.

Q. Known as the City of Children, Mooseheart is owned and operated by what organization?

A. The Loyal Order of Moose, which provides for orphans and other dependent children there.

Q. Iowa-born John L. Lewis, longtime head of the United Mine Workers Union, was a resident in what two Illinois towns?

A. Panama and Springfield.

Q. What was the projected cost to build the Drake Hotel at Lake Shore Drive and Oak in 1914?

A. Two million dollars.

Q. What is the name of the motor route through Kentucky, Indiana, and Illinois, which covers 2,500 miles of Lincoln landmarks?

A. Lincoln Heritage Trail.

Q. For what Illinoisan is the town of Saint Joseph named?

A. Joseph Kelly, a pre-Civil War tavern keeper who was the first postmaster.

Q. What is the only part of Illinois that lies west of the Mississippi River?

A. Kaskaskia Island.

Q. A race riot in what Illinois city in 1908 led directly to the founding of the National Association for the Advancement of Colored People?

A. Springfield.

Q. What expression meaning that a political campaign has appeal for solid middle-class citizens pinpoints the name of an Illinois city?

A. "It'll play in Peoria."

ENTERTAINMENT

C H A P T E R   T W O

Q. Where was Jack Benny born?

A. Waukegan, on Valentine's Day, 1894.

———◆———

Q. David Ogden Stiers, who played Charles Emerson Winchester III on the television series "M*A*S*H," was born in what Illinois town?

A. Peoria.

———◆———

Q. Comic performer John Belushi and the team of Mike Nichols and Elaine May were launched professionally at what cabaret theater serving biting satire and improvisation?

A. Second City, Chicago.

———◆———

Q. What kept residents along the Stony Island streetcar route awake late August 19, 1896?

A. A party with sixty-four trolley cars, two bands, and four thousand Royal League members.

———◆———

Q. What order concerning their personal entertainment did Cardinal Mundelein issue to Chicago priests in June 1916?

A. He forbade them to attend the theater.

Q. What Chicago ordinance, effective August 29, 1913, affected restaurants?

A. Public dancing was forbidden there.

Q. What Oak Park actress and comedienne is a sit-com veteran and advocate for animal rights?

A. Betty White.

Q. What Chicago native starred in the movies *Alien Nation* and the *Princess Bride*?

A. Mandy Patinkin.

Q. The actor DeWolf Hopper, appearing in *El Capitan* at the Columbia Theater in January 1898, almost caused a riot by refusing to perform what recitation?

A. The poem "Casey at the Bat."

Q. What Chicago actress played Vanessa Huxtable on the popular television comedy "The Cosby Show"?

A. Tempestt Bledsoe.

Q. In 1912, the manager of the dance pavilion at Sans Souci Park characterized what music as "worse than alcohol" for young people?

A. Ragtime.

Q. What Chicagoan was the lead singer for the sixties rock group Jefferson Airplane, later Jefferson Starship?

A. Grace Slick.

Q. What Elgin native starred in the Disney movie *Tron*, among others?

A. Bruce Boxleitner.

———◆———

Q. How many cars were on display in 1912 at the Eleventh Annual Auto Show in the Chicago Coliseum?

A. Four hundred, priced from $350 to $8,000.

———◆———

Q. What stand-up comedian and veteran actor of movies, including *Silver Streak* and *Hear No Evil, See No Evil*, was born in Peoria?

A. Richard Pryor.

———◆———

Q. The Union League Club's members paid how much per plate for the annual "game dinner" at the Grand Pacific Hotel in December 1909?

A. Seven dollars.

———◆———

Q. Where was Susan Dey, star of the television show "L.A. Law" and the once-popular "Partridge Family," born?

A. Pekin.

———◆———

Q. For how much did Lloyd's of London insure the drum-beating hands of Gene Krupa, a Chicago native who became a professional musician at age seventeen?

A. $100,000.

———◆———

Q. What actor from Chicago is greeted by shouts of "Norm!" whenever he enters the bar on the television series "Cheers"?

A. George Wendt.

Q. What singer from Chicago made famous such hits as "Jezebel" and "Mule Train"?

A. Frankie Laine.

———◆———

Q. What regular Chicago television show did Norman Ross host?

A. "Off the Cuff."

———◆———

Q. Marlin Perkins, long-time director of Chicago's Lincoln Park Zoo, hosted what two popular television shows?

A. "Zoo Parade" and "Wild Kingdom."

———◆———

Q. What Chicago-born president of the American Federation of Musicians had his greatest victory as a labor leader in 1942 when he forced recording companies to pay a royalty to the musicians for every recording they sold?

A. James C. Petrillo, president from 1940 to 1958 and president of the Chicago branch of the Union until 1963.

———◆———

Q. What Chicago-born actor "never leaves home without it"?

A. Karl Malden.

———◆———

Q. Why did Dr. Melbourne E. Boynton of Chicago's Woodlawn Baptist Church, in June 1914 urge all ministers to resign from private clubs?

A. He declared private clubs more dangerous than saloons.

———◆———

Q. Why did the nation's dancing masters, meeting in Chicago in September 1912, campaign against ragtime music?

A. Because its syncopation was inimical to dancing, they believed.

Q. Pop/folk singer Dan Fogelberg was born in what town?

A. Peoria.

———————◆———————

Q. Tom Bosley, who had roles in the television shows "Charlie's Angels," "Happy Days," and "Father Dowling," was born in what city?

A. Chicago.

———————◆———————

Q. What Hunt Township native played Big Daddy in the movie *Cat On A Hot Tin Roof*?

A. Burl Ives.

———————◆———————

Q. What annual event takes place in Springfield at the end of June?

A. The two-day Lincolnfest.

———————◆———————

Q. On January 24, 1897, how many policemen were needed for crowd control at the National Cycle Show at the Coliseum in Chicago?

A. 340.

———————◆———————

Q. New Rochelle native Peter Scolari starred with Tom Hanks on what television sit-com?

A. "Bosom Buddies."

———————◆———————

Q. Where did Redd Foxx, the television sitcom star who died in 1991, first come into prominence?

A. The Regal Theater on Chicago's South Side.

Q. When was the first theater license issued in Chicago?

A. October 1837, with admission priced at seventy-five cents.

Q. What was the name of the character that Chicago-born Ken Olin played on the prime-time show "thirtysomething"?

A. Michael Steadman.

Q. Why were police called July 30, 1917, to the Oak Street beach?

A. Several thousand angry persons insisted they had as much right to the beach as residents of the Gold Coast.

Q. What Rock Island native starred with Ava Gabor on the television show "Green Acres"?

A. Eddie Albert.

Q. What St. Anne rural mail carrier is believed to have the largest collection of James Bond memorabilia in the world?

A. Doug Redenius.

Q. Once a leading man in the movies and later a star of the television show "My Three Sons," Fred MacMurray was born in what Illinois town?

A. Kankakee.

Q. What silent screen actress starred in a "sensational movie" at Chicago's Ziegfeld Theater in April 1915?

A. Theda Bara, in *A Fool There Was*.

ENTERTAINMENT

Q. What motion picture did Mayor Thompson order banned in Chicago in May 1915?

A. *The Birth of a Nation.*

———◆———

Q. Chicagoan and veteran comedian Harvey Korman was a long-running cast member of what television series?

A. "The Carol Burnett Show."

———◆———

Q. Why did Chicago authorities warn that at least eighty theaters, most of them nickelodeons, might not have their licenses renewed in 1912?

A. For failure to obey safety regulations.

———◆———

Q. What record did the Chicago post office set on February 14, 1908?

A. There were 2,696,642 valentines mailed in twenty-four hours.

———◆———

Q. What young Chicago actress has starred in many films including *Splash*, *Roxanne*, and *Steel Magnolias*?

A. Darryl Hannah.

———◆———

Q. The annual masquerade ball of what professional group was held in December 1908 at Turner Hall on the North Side?

A. Chicago chefs and cooks.

———◆———

Q. Great Lakes native rhythm and blues artist Chaka Khan was born with what name?

A. Yvette Stevens.

Q. How did eighty members of the Chicago Automobile Club celebrate New Year's Day, 1909?

A. By making a 100-mile drive to Aurora and Elgin and back.

◆

Q. What native of Christopher, Illinois, starred with Glenn Close in the Academy Award-winning film *Dangerous Liaisons*?

A. John Malkovich.

◆

Q. What did the opening of the bock beer season accomplish in Chicago on April 18, 1908?

A. Twenty-five barrels were consumed.

◆

Q. When were boys and girls first permitted to swim in the same pool at Chicago's South Park, if their parents were present?

A. May 1908.

◆

Q. How did ten-year-old Illinoisan Anna Chlumsky become famous in autumn 1991?

A. By co-starring in the movie *My Girl*, with Macaulay Culkin.

◆

Q. Octogenarian Milt Hinton, who took 25,000 photographs of his fellow musicians during the time he played bass with Cab Calloway and others, compiled his reminiscences into what book in 1988?

A. *Bass Line: The Stories and Photographs of Milt Hinton*.

◆

Q. What Rockford native has appeared in such television series as "Roseanne," "Who's the Boss," "Dallas," and "Knots Landing"?

A. Andrea Walters.

Q. The Gate of Horn, a former Chicago nightclub, had what slogan?

A. The Nightclub for People Who Hate Nightclubs.

———◆———

Q. What tournament chess player and jazz record fan is president of the Boys and Girls Clubs of Chicago?

A. Robert K. Hassin, the first black to hold the position.

———◆———

Q. Chicagoan Lawrence Tero, who had a supporting role in *Rocky II* and starred in the television show "The A-Team," goes by what nickname?

A. Mr. T.

———◆———

Q. How many gorillas does the Lincoln Park Zoological Gardens have?

A. Twenty-nine at the zoo, with nine others out for breeding purposes, more than any other zoo in the country.

———◆———

Q. What two nationally known women telecasters moved to the network level from Chicago?

A. Jane Pauley and Deborah Norville.

———◆———

Q. Where do rail buffs from across the nation get their kicks in Illinois?

A. Union, where one can ride on interurban cars, street-cars, diesel and steam trains.

———◆———

Q. How many persons visit the popular Chicago Historical Society annually?

A. More than two hundred thousand.

Q. What son of a Normal physician, who played Lt. Col. Henry Blake on the television show "M*A*S*H," is the unpaid national spokesman for the Children's National Burn Foundation in Sherman Oaks, California?

A. McLean Stevenson.

———◆———

Q. Who starred in *Graustark*, the film made from G. B. McCutcheon's novel, at the Fine Arts Theater in 1915?

A. Beverly Bayne and Francis X. Bushman.

———◆———

Q. In 1909, how did the Abraham Lincoln Center in Chicago celebrate the centennial of Lincoln's birth?

A. With a Calico Dance, all attending wearing the garb of 1809.

———◆———

Q. What 1914 ordinance did Chicago clubwomen intend to combat?

A. One legalizing tea-dances in Loop hotels and restaurants.

———◆———

Q. In what city was Charlton Heston, star of the 1959 movie *Ben Hur* and other films, born?

A. Evanston.

———◆———

Q. What actor, who starred in the television series "Marcus Welby, M.D." as well as many movies, was born in Chicago in 1907?

A. Robert Young.

———◆———

Q. Where was John Sturgis, who directed *Bad Day at Black Rock* and dozens of other movies, born?

A. Oak Park.

ENTERTAINMENT

Q. What was the admission to attend the Chicago park district's show *Holiday Wonders* in December 1991?

A. A donation of clothing, canned goods, shoes, or winter coats to help the homeless.

Q. "Bozo's Circus," directed or produced by Allen Hall for most of its 30-year run at WGN-TV, ended an 11-year backlog of reservations in 1990. What was done then?

A. A telephone lottery was held on St. Patrick's Day, 1991, and 125,000 tickets allotted to those who reached the station. 17,000,000 calls were placed during the 5-hour period.

Q. What Elmhurst plumbing contractor tried to have St. Patrick's Day declared a national holiday?

A. Edward Martin Moran.

Q. What La Grange-born musician and composer organized the Modern Jazz Quartet and pioneered in the development of Third Stream Music?

A. John Aaron Lewis.

Q. Where was film director Vincente Minnelli, husband of Judy Garland and father of Liza Minnelli, born?

A. Chicago.

Q. What comedian from Oak Park, with stand-up routines and television shows to his credit, won a Grammy Award for his album *Button Down Mind* in 1960?

A. Bob Newhart.

Q. What blues singer, known for his powerful voice, died in an accident shortly before New Year's Day, 1991?

A. Andrew ("B.B.") Odom, who settled in Chicago in 1960.

Q. What former movie star gave the Museum of Science and Industry the amazing Fairy Castle, a dollhouse which cost almost half a million dollars when it was built in the 1920s?

A. Colleen Moore, who married Homer Hargrave, a Chicago stockbroker, in the mid-1930s.

———◆———

Q. What well-known Manhattan pianist-singer was born in Danville in 1936 and had only a few weeks of piano lessons, but has played at Carnegie Hall?

A. Bobby Short.

———◆———

Q. Illinois's oldest radio station, WDZ in Decatur, started in Tuscola in what year?

A. 1921.

———◆———

Q. Famed actor Joseph Jefferson III and his theatrical company performed at what unusual place in Pekin in 1838?

A. A "porkhouse," whose occupants disrupted the show with porcine noises.

———◆———

Q. What entrepreneur spent $85,000 in 1857 to build the third theater in Chicago?

A. John H. McVicker.

———◆———

Q. What musical group drew a standing-room crowd to a performance in the Springfield courthouse in 1853?

A. The Swiss Bell Ringers.

———◆———

Q. In the 1890s, what were popular venues for entertainment along the Mississippi and Illinois rivers?

A. "Floating theaters," or showboats.

Q. *Ordinary People* is one of many movie credits for what Evanston actress?

A. Elizabeth McGovern.

———◆———

Q. In what theaters did the Federal Theater perform in Chicago during the Great Depression?

A. The Blackstone and the Great Northern.

———◆———

Q. The state's first commercial television station, WBBM-TV, began broadcasting in Chicago in what year?

A. 1940.

———◆———

Q. How large was the Ferris wheel at the World's Columbian Exposition?

A. 250 feet in diameter, accommodating 2,160 riders.

———◆———

Q. In 1922, what young New Orleans jazz trumpeter moved to Chicago to play in the band of Joe ("King") Oliver, two years later joining Fletcher Henderson's band?

A. Louis Armstrong.

———◆———

Q. What Chicago Hyde Park High School senior left school to tour with a band?

A. Mel Torme.

———◆———

Q. What group offers nostalgic trips to Chicago's famed gangster-related spots, including Capone's "office," the St. Valentine's massacre scene, Dillinger's shooting by G-men, and others?

A. Untouchable Tours.

Q. What influential Chicagoan suggested holding a country music festival in mid-1991, the first of an annual series?

A. Mayor Richard Daley, who is said to be a country music buff.

◆

Q. What Chicago actor has had roles on both the television show "Hill Street Blues" and the recent movie hit *Die Hard 2*?

A. Dennis Franz.

◆

Q. Why did Chicago police halt the showing of *The Spirit of '76* on May 14, 1917?

A. It was regarded as anti-British.

◆

Q. What evangelist proposed in 1911 that, since all who engaged in mixed dancing were "galloping gaily to perdition," boys should dance with boys and girls with girls?

A. H. H. Van Meter.

◆

Q. What two Peoria residents comprised the famous radio team of Fibber McGee and Molly?

A. Jim Jordan and Marian Driscoll, husband and wife.

◆

Q. Who was the first jazz pianist to appear at Chicago's Orchestra Hall?

A. Dorothy Donegan, in 1942.

◆

Q. When Buffalo Bill and his Wild West show reached Chicago July 24, 1898, how large was the troupe?

A. 680 people and 700 horses.

Q. What Pembroke-born stand-up comedian co-authored the musical revue, *Do the White Thing*?

A. Aaron Freeman, in collaboration with Bob Kolson.

———◆———

Q. According to a recent poll of 161 art museums in the nation, where does the Art Institute of Chicago rank in attendance?

A. Third, behind the National Gallery of Art and the Metropolitan Museum.

———◆———

Q. How many persons are employed at Six Flags Great America on an average day in summer?

A. About three thousand.

———◆———

Q. Shelley Berman, Paul Newman, Tom Bosley, and Geraldine Page were among what group that put on sixteen shows a season at the Opera House in the 1950s?

A. Woodstock Players.

———◆———

Q. What attorney persuaded Springfield authorities to waive a prohibitive license fee so that the Joseph Jefferson dramatic troupe could appear there in the late 1830s?

A. Abraham Lincoln.

———◆———

Q. What pair of "firsts" did the Beaubien brothers share in 1834?

A. Mark owned Chicago's first fiddle and John the first piano.

———◆———

Q. What Highland Park native played the father of six children on the sit-com "The Brady Bunch"?

A. Robert Reed.

Q. Who was the Midwest's representative at the Miss Chinese International Pageant in January 1991 in Hong Kong?

A. Alyna Chien, who has a University of Chicago degree in East Asian languages and was chosen Miss Friendship Ambassador in a Chinatown contest.

Q. What unusual way of seeing Chicago is offered from Meigs Field?

A. Helicopter rides.

Q. What new endeavor did Betty Thomas, who went from Second City to "Hill Street Blues," plan for 1992?

A. Directing a motion picture, *Only You*.

Q. What musician and band leader, known as the King of Percussion, who died in Oak Park in December 1991, appeared with such musicians as Arturo Toscanini, Diana Ross, Guy Lombardo, and Perry Como during his long career?

A. Bobby Christian.

Q. What Chicago native was the long-time head of the CBS network?

A. William S. Paley.

Q. What did a group in Moline do in 1870 to raise funds for a public library?

A. Held a strawberry festival.

Q. Who recorded "The Death of Mother Jones" in 1932, commemorating the fiery union organizer?

A. A little-known singer, Gene Autry.

Q. What Evanston-born actor portrayed Father Mulcahy on the television series "M*A*S*H"?

A. William Christopher.

Q. What blues singer, who began her career in Chicago, married Richard ("Night Train") Lane, a defensive back with the Chicago Cardinals and future Hall of Famer?

A. Dinah Washington.

Q. The Chicago River provided what wintertime diversion for Chicago residents in the 1830s?

A. Ice-skating.

Q. What Evanston actress won a Tony award for her performance in the drama *The Apple Tree*?

A. Barbara Harris.

Q. What was unusual about a fund-raising affair held at the Four Seasons in Chicago October 21, 1991, for the benefit of the hungry?

A. Those attending the "Dinner without Dinner" were entertained, but served nothing but water.

Q. Why was the multi-talented Steve Allen in Chicago in late October 1991?

A. As guest of honor at a dinner at the Museum of Broadcast Communications.

Q. What Danville native plays Luther on the sit-com "Coach"?

A. Jerry Van Dyke.

Q. How did the Chicago city council improve the city's many saloons in March 1919?

A. They were ordered to remove their "Family Entrance" signs.

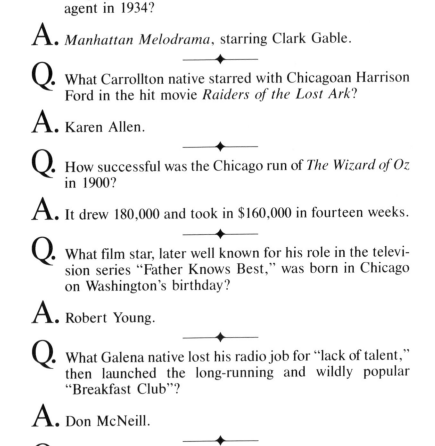

Q. What movie did gangster John Dillinger see at Chicago's Biograph Theatre just before he was killed by an F.B.I. agent in 1934?

A. *Manhattan Melodrama*, starring Clark Gable.

Q. What Carrollton native starred with Chicagoan Harrison Ford in the hit movie *Raiders of the Lost Ark*?

A. Karen Allen.

Q. How successful was the Chicago run of *The Wizard of Oz* in 1900?

A. It drew 180,000 and took in $160,000 in fourteen weeks.

Q. What film star, later well known for his role in the television series "Father Knows Best," was born in Chicago on Washington's birthday?

A. Robert Young.

Q. What Galena native lost his radio job for "lack of talent," then launched the long-running and wildly popular "Breakfast Club"?

A. Don McNeill.

Q. Actress Donna Mills of Chicago is best known for her role in what prime-time drama?

A. "Knots Landing."

Q. In 1912, an attempt was made in Chicago to ban the showing of what play by the Irish dramatist John Millington Synge because of indecency and immorality?

A. *The Playboy of the Western World.*

———◆———

Q. What veteran movie actor from Chicago had starring roles in *Platoon* and *The Big Chill*?

A. Tom Berenger.

———◆———

Q. What television show did Bergen Evans, Northwestern University professor, host?

A. "Down You Go."

———◆———

Q. Where was Mel Torme, a.k.a. the Velvet Fog, born?

A. Chicago, September 13, 1925.

———◆———

Q. What did one member of the new board of movie censors say in 1914?

A. That only films suitable for children's viewing should be approved.

———◆———

Q. In what Illinois city was "NBC Nightly News" commentator John Chancellor born?

A. Chicago.

———◆———

Q. In the early days of motion pictures, in what Chicago studio were a large share of the nation's movies filmed?

A. The Essanay Studios on the North Side.

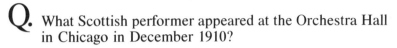

Q. What Scottish performer appeared at the Orchestra Hall in Chicago in December 1910?

A. Harry Lauder.

———◆———

Q. What actor, whose hometown was Gillespie, made his stage debut in *Carousel* and later starred in other musicals including *Kiss Me Kate* and *Showboat*?

A. Howard Keel.

———◆———

Q. Bill Murray, original cast member of "Saturday Night Live" and star of such movies as *Stripes* and *Scrooged*, is from what town?

A. Evanston.

———◆———

Q. Whose band played at the opening of the Empire Room at the Palmer House many years ago?

A. Jules Herbuveaux, a saxophonist, who later managed Channel 5, WMAQ, and was an NBC vice president.

———◆———

Q. At what age did Nat ("King") Cole become a Chicagoan?

A. Age four, when his father, a clergyman, moved there.

———◆———

Q. In what city was Pat Sajac, host of the game show "Wheel of Fortune" and the late night talk show "The Pat Sajac Show," born?

A. Chicago.

———◆———

Q. By what name was Louella Oettinger of Freeport famous?

A. Louella Parsons, Hollywood gossip columnist.

Q. What jazz clarinetist, the King of Swing in the 1930s, was born in Chicago, played in Hull House as a child, and formed his first band in the Windy City?

A. Benny Goodman.

———◆———

Q. What Chicago-born actor has such movies to his credit as *Star Wars*, *Raiders of the Lost Ark*, *Presumed Innocent*, *Witness*, and *Regarding Henry*?

A. Harrison Ford.

———◆———

Q. What dances did the Saddle & Cycle Club ban in 1912?

A. Grizzly Bear, Turkey Trot, and Bunny Hug.

———◆———

Q. What was the name of the 1970s hit television series starring Chicago native actor/singer David Soul?

A. "Starsky and Hutch".

———◆———

Q. Why did Joseph Dunton, member of the board of Lincoln Park, request more Negro melodies and less classical music in 1898?

A. He said Wagner was boring.

———◆———

Q. What Christopher native was host of the popular game show "Match Game"?

A. Gene Rayburn.

———◆———

Q. Chicago *Sun-Times* columnist Irv Kupcinet was once host for what television show?

A. "At Random."

Q. What Ft. Sheridan-born actor played Chuck Yeager in the film *The Right Stuff*?

A. Sam Shepard.

———◆———

Q. Where did comedic actor Steve Allen attend high school?

A. Chicago's Hyde Park.

———◆———

Q. What play opened at the Studebaker Theater in Chicago on Christmas night, 1909?

A. *Alias Jimmy Valentine*, adapted from a short story by O. Henry.

———◆———

Q. Comedic actor George Wendt narrates the promotional video for what Chicago stadium?

A. New Comiskey Park.

———◆———

Q. How old is Chicagoan Etta Moten Barnett, former singer and dancer, who appeared on Broadway and in the movies?

A. She turned ninety in 1991.

———◆———

Q. Mary Gross, comedienne on "Saturday Night Live," and Michael Gross, star of the sit-com "Family Ties," are brother and sister from what Illinois city?

A. Chicago.

———◆———

Q. Buddy Ebsen, who played Jed Clampett on the "Beverly Hillbillies," was born in what town?

A. Belleville.

Q. What two-person, two-puppet television show was one of the most popular ever?

A. "Kukla, Fran, and Ollie", created by Chicagoan Burr Tillstrom.

Q. What Park Ridge actress had a role in the classic film *Come Back to the Five and Dime, Jimmy Dean, Jimmy Dean*?

A. Karen Black.

Q. Who succeeded Claudia Cassidy as the dean of Chicago drama critics?

A. Richard Christiansen of the *Tribune*, a critic of the theater for thirty years.

Q. Who was co-founder of the renowned Steppenwolf Theater company in Chicago?

A. John Malkovich.

Q. What Northwestern University student returned to classes after starring in the movie *The Father of the Bride*?

A. Kimberly Williams.

Q. What well-known actress is a regular on the television show "Roseanne"?

A. Laurie Metcalfe, a Second City alumna.

Q. What son of a Chicago advertising man played the role of Franklin D. Roosevelt in the Broadway play *Sunrise at Campobello*?

A. Ralph Bellamy.

Q. What is the date of the first amateur theatrical production in Illinois?

A. December 3, 1836, in Springfield.

Q. What Chicago actor co-starred with William Shatner on the television series "T. J. Hooker"?

A. Adrian Zmed.

Q. Where did John Philip Sousa and his band perform for one night in Chicago February 2, 1895?

A. Hooley's Theater.

Q. What actor, a Windy City native, starred in *The Iceman Cometh* and *A Thousand Clowns*?

A. Jason Robards.

Q. For what occasion did five thousand people attend a talk on the Victorian Era in Chicago's Auditorium June 22, 1897?

A. Queen Victoria's Diamond Jubilee.

Q. In what Illinois city is the only zoo in the country where dolphin shows can be seen?

A. Brookfield.

Q. What Chicago-born actress co-starred with James Stewart in the movie *Vertigo*?

A. Kim Novak.

ENTERTAINMENT

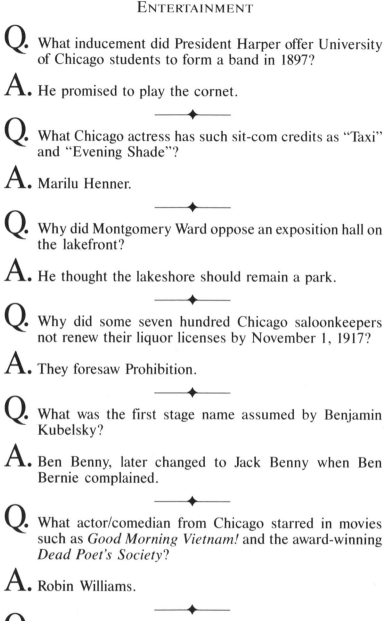

Q. What inducement did President Harper offer University of Chicago students to form a band in 1897?

A. He promised to play the cornet.

Q. What Chicago actress has such sit-com credits as "Taxi" and "Evening Shade"?

A. Marilu Henner.

Q. Why did Montgomery Ward oppose an exposition hall on the lakefront?

A. He thought the lakeshore should remain a park.

Q. Why did some seven hundred Chicago saloonkeepers not renew their liquor licenses by November 1, 1917?

A. They foresaw Prohibition.

Q. What was the first stage name assumed by Benjamin Kubelsky?

A. Ben Benny, later changed to Jack Benny when Ben Bernie complained.

Q. What actor/comedian from Chicago starred in movies such as *Good Morning Vietnam!* and the award-winning *Dead Poet's Society*?

A. Robin Williams.

Q. What Zion-born actor is noted for his undersized stature and starring role on the sit-com "Different Strokes"?

A. Gary Coleman.

Q. What patriotic song, popular in the Civil War, was introduced by Chicago singer Jules Lumbard and his brother Frank?

A. "The Battle Cry of Freedom."

Q. Comedienne and character actress Carol Lawrence was born in what Illinois town?

A. Melrose Park.

Q. Who were the three co-founders of the famous Second City in December 1959?

A. Paul Sills, Bernie Sahlins, and Howard Alk.

Q. What veteran performer from Chicago recently toured the nation in the lead role of *Hello Dolly*?

A. Mitzi Gaynor.

Q. Who is the owner of the Candlelight Dinner Playhouse in Summit?

A. Bill Pullinsi.

Q. Chicago native Martin Mull starred in what 1970s hit television series?

A. "Mary Hartman, Mary Hartman".

Q. What cult movie director, with credits including *Animal House*, *Blues Brothers*, and *Amazon Women on the Moon*, is from Chicago?

A. John Landis.

Q. Chicago-born Karl Malden, who starred in the movies *Streets of San Francisco* and *On the Waterfront*, was born with what name?

A. Malden Sekulovich.

———◆———

Q. What Joliet native won the Miss America contest in 1927?

A. Lois Delaner.

———◆———

Q. The tricentennial celebration in 1980 of Peoria's founding was marked by a year-long series of events concluding with what highlight?

A. The All-Star Celebrity Homecoming, with invitations sent to Richard Pryor, Jack Brickhouse, Faith Daniels, Sam Kinison, Bob Jamieson, and others.

———◆———

Q. What is the seating capacity of the Arie Crown Theater in McCormick Place?

A. 4,319.

———◆———

Q. Where was Clayton Moore, famous for his portrayal of the Lone Ranger, born?

A. Chicago.

———◆———

Q. What was Gillespie native Howard Keel's name before he changed it for the stage?

A. Howard Leek.

———◆———

Q. What well-known Quincy actress got her start in the silent films?

A. Mary Astor.

Q. How long did Joe ("Roosting Joe") Powers remain atop the Morrison Hotel flagpole in July 1927?

A. Sixteen days, two hours, and forty-five minutes.

———◆———

Q. What Chicago native wrote the screenplay for *Butch Cassidy and the Sundance Kid*, starring Robert Redford and Paul Newman?

A. William Goldman.

———◆———

Q. What happened after comedian Dick Gregory was persuaded by Jack Paar to appear on his TV show?

A. Gregory's pay for a week-long job jumped from $250 to $5,000 in less than a month.

———◆———

Q. What comedic actor from Moline has had roles in the sitcoms "Mayberry R.F.D." and "Mama's Family"?

A. Ken Berry.

———◆———

Q. What do the call letters of the Chicago public television station, WTTW, stand for?

A. Window to the World.

———◆———

Q. What veteran movie actor from Chicago starred in the film *Silent Running*?

A. Bruce Dern.

———◆———

Q. For what two television series is Chicagoan Robert Conrad best known?

A. "Baa Baa Black Sheep" and "Wild Wild West."

Q. Who was among the performers responsible for creating the free-and-easy style that marked early Chicago television?

A. The late Dave Garroway.

Q. What television comic from Chicago had a role in the series "The Dick Van Dyke Show?"

A. Morey Amsterdam.

Q. At what Chicago museum can visitors anchor a newscast, then purchase the videotape of the show?

A. Museum of Broadcast Communications.

Q. Barbara Hale, who played Della Street on "The Perry Mason Show," was born in what Illinois town?

A. De Kalb.

Q. What veteran film actor from Chicago has had roles in such movies as *The Concrete Jungle*, *The Spy Who Came in from the Cold*, and the recent *Guilty by Suspicion*?

A. Sam Wanamaker.

Q. What musical had a record run of four years at the Apollo Theater in Chicago?

A. *Pump Boys and Dinettes*.

Q. What Chicago-born singer had a number one hit with his song "You'll Never Find Another Love Like Mine"?

A. Lou Rawls.

Q. Who infuriated TV executives by calling television "a vast wasteland" when he was head of the FCC some thirty years ago?

A. Attorney Newton Minow, a graduate of Northwestern University.

———◆———

Q. Chicagoan William Friedkin directed what popular horror film of the 1970s?

A. *The Exorcist.*

———◆———

Q. What famous Chicago choreographer wrote and directed the autobiographical movie *All That Jazz*?

A. Bob Fosse.

———◆———

Q. What did Joe Tinker, the Cubs shortstop, do on January 10, 1909?

A. Made his stage debut at the Haymarket Theater with a role in *A Great Catch*.

———◆———

Q. What Evanston-born actress had roles in the movies *Plaza Suite* and *Nashville*?

A. Barbara Harris.

———◆———

Q. Multi-instrumentalist, jazz/pop performer Herbie Hancock was born in what Illinois city?

A. Chicago.

———◆———

Q. What Chicago-born playwright wrote the film script for *The Postman Always Rings Twice*, and whose first play, *Sexual Perversity in Chicago* (1977), was made into the movie *About Last Night* in the 1980s?

A. David Mamet.

HISTORY

C H A P T E R   T H R E E

Q. How many Illinois men fought in the Civil War?

A. About 257,000.

---◆---

Q. What legendary frontier scout and peace officer, who was shot to death in a saloon in Deadwood, Dakota Territory, was born in Troy Grove?

A. Wild Bill Hickok.

---◆---

Q. The work of what social reformer in 1892 led to an Illinois factory law limiting women's working hours and prohibiting child labor?

A. Florence Kelley.

---◆---

Q. What revived the failing University of Chicago in 1889?

A. John D. Rockefeller's gift of $600,000.

---◆---

Q. On what date did the Great Chicago Fire begin?

A. October 8, 1871.

Q. What Chicago manicurist was the first black person to earn a pilot's license?

A. Bessie Coleman.

Q. What was the outcome when Clarence Darrow, famed Chicago attorney, was accused of trying to bribe a juror in a Los Angeles dynamite case?

A. Darrow was acquitted.

Q. What were women delegates to the 1912 Republican Convention in Chicago ordered to do?

A. Remain hatless.

Q. How many Chicago mayors were murdered in office?

A. Two: Carter H. Harrison, Sr., and Anton J. Cermak.

Q. How many died when the steamer *Lady Elgin* sank in Lake Michigan near Evanston the night of September 7, 1860?

A. 293.

Q. How long did Illinoisan Mary Ann ("Mother") Bickerdyke serve as a Civil War relief worker?

A. Four years, starting at the Union Hospital in Cairo.

Q. Who assassinated Chicago mayor Anton J. Cermak?

A. Giuseppe Zangara, a mentally ill bricklayer who wanted to kill a "great ruler" and was aiming at Franklin D. Roosevelt.

Q. How did the Indians describe the first sailing vessels they saw on Lake Michigan?

A. "Canoes-with-wings."

———◆———

Q. Who shot Chicago mayor Carter H. Harrison?

A. A disappointed office-seeker during the 1893 exposition.

———◆———

Q. What Garrett Biblical Institute student helped rescue seventeen people from the sinking *Lady Elgin* before collapsing from exhaustion?

A. Edward Spencer.

———◆———

Q. In 1832, when Indians attacked Apple River Fort near what is now Elizabeth, who saved the fort in the absence of male defenders?

A. Mrs. Elizabeth Armstrong, who rallied the few defenders.

———◆———

Q. What well-known Chicagoan was an outstanding authority on Abraham Lincoln?

A. Paul Angle, head of the Chicago Historical Society.

———◆———

Q. According to legend, the Great Chicago Fire was started when a cow kicked over a lighted lantern in the barn belonging to what person?

A. Mrs. Patrick O'Leary.

———◆———

Q. What office had Edward F. Dunne held before being named governor in 1913?

A. Mayor of Chicago.

Q. What father and son were governors of Illinois?

A. Richard Yates, during the Civil War, and Richard Yates, Jr., in 1900.

◆

Q. When Anton Cermak was murdered in 1933, how many extra papers about the shooting did the Chicago *Tribune* sell?

A. 188,602.

◆

Q. What did Dr. Benjamin Franklin Stevenson, a Civil War surgeon, do on April 6, 1866?

A. Organized the Grand Army of the Republic, a society of Union veterans, in Decatur.

◆

Q. What disappointed office-seeker from Chicago fatally shot Pres. James A. Garfield in 1881?

A. Attorney Charles J. Guiteau.

◆

Q. When did Evanston native Frances E. Willard, founder of the Women's Christian Temperance Union, die?

A. 1898.

◆

Q. What explanation did Big Jim O'Leary, gambler and saloon-keeper, give for the 1871 Chicago fire in his mother's barn?

A. Spontaneous combustion of green hay.

◆

Q. Why did Henry Ford sue the Chicago *Tribune* in 1916?

A. The paper called him an anarchist; Ford won damages of six cents in 1919 and received a letter of apology from the publisher, Robert R. McCormick, July 30, 1941, their mutual birthday.

Q. When Jack Thompson of the Chicago *Tribune* made parachute jumps in North Africa and Sicily in 1942 and 1943, why did he land in the record books?

A. He was the first war correspondent to jump in combat.

——◆——

Q. When did Archbishop George W. Mundelein succeed Archbishop James E. Quigley in Chicago?

A. February 8, 1916.

——◆——

Q. What happened when a Chicago & Northwestern express jumped the tracks at Howard Street in December 1909?

A. Two passengers died and eighteen were injured.

——◆——

Q. Why did Dr. W. A. Evans, Chicago health commissioner, suggest that his annual salary of $8,000 be cut by 10 percent in December 1909?

A. So the $800 saved could be used to raise other salaries.

——◆——

Q. Orville T. Bright, a Chicago district superintendent of schools, lashed out at whom in January 1910?

A. Teachers who urged kindness to animals but wore feathers on their hats.

——◆——

Q. Why did forty thousand people turn out in Chicago's Grant Park on August 16, 1913, as part of a nationwide celebration?

A. It was the 100th anniversary of Lt. Oliver Hazard Perry's victory at the battle of Lake Erie.

——◆——

Q. What Chicago native was secretary of state under presidents Franklin D. Roosevelt and Harry Truman?

A. Edward R. Stettinius, Jr.

Q. When the United States entered World War I, what army division was furnished entirely by Illinois, one of only four states to furnish men for an entire army division?

A. The Thirty-third, or Prairie Division.

✦

Q. What two sets of fathers and sons were mayors of Chicago?

A. Carter H. Harrison and Carter Harrison, Jr.; Richard J. Daley and Richard M. Daley.

✦

Q. Whom did President Taft name in 1912 as chief of the Children's Bureau?

A. Julia Lathrop of Rockford, the first woman to head a federal committee.

✦

Q. What first black priest in the United States died in Chicago in 1897 while serving as pastor of Saint Monica's Church?

A. Fr. Augustine Tolton, born of slave parents, ordained in Rome in 1886.

✦

Q. Which one of Lincoln's teachers is buried near Huntsville?

A. Azel Waters Dorsey, who taught Lincoln for six months in Indiana in 1824.

✦

Q. What Springfield native served as president of the Pullman Company in 1897-1911?

A. Robert Todd Lincoln, son of Abraham Lincoln.

✦

Q. When did the Chicago stockyards open?

A. 1865.

Q. On what date did an electric streetcar make its first trip in Chicago?

A. December 2, 1895, on Clark Street.

———◆———

Q. Author George Ade and others auctioned thirty-four boxes for the 1909 annual charity ball, raising how much?

A. $23,800.

———◆———

Q. What employee benefit plan did Sears, Roebuck announce on July 1, 1916?

A. Profit-sharing, to which it would contribute $500,000 annually.

———◆———

Q. What did school authorities estimate Chicago's population to be in July 1916?

A. 2.55 million, an increase of 365,000 since the 1910 census.

———◆———

Q. How many men of draft age did Chicago police and government agents pick up in a citywide sweep July 11, 1918?

A. 5,000, of whom 1,137 were draft dodgers or unregistered aliens.

———◆———

Q. Why were four members of the Chicago Symphony Orchestra questioned by an assistant district attorney on August 9, 1918?

A. For allegedly making "un-American statements."

———◆———

Q. What Civil War general, who was born in Jackson County, represented Illinois in the U.S. House and Senate after the war and is credited with naming May 30, 1868, as the first Memorial Day?

A. John Alexander Logan.

Q. How many autos were stolen in Chicago during the first seven months of 1916?

A. A world record of 2,600, ten times as many as in New York.

———◆———

Q. What did the sixty-eight teachers and principals fired by the Chicago Board of Education in June 1916 have in common?

A. All belonged to the Chicago Teachers Federation.

———◆———

Q. The wearing of only "one rat, one ring, and one fancy pin" was stipulated in the dress code of what Chicago business in 1909?

A. Marshall Field's.

———◆———

Q. What Illinois native, born on a farm near Shawneetown, was in charge of the troops who captured Confederate president Jefferson Davis after Appomattox?

A. James H. Wilson, who had served as a cavalry commander under General Sherman.

———◆———

Q. Who was the most heavily insured person in Chicago in 1912?

A. Mrs. Charles Netcher, Boston store owner, $1.3 million.

———◆———

Q. When did the last of the fruit stands have to move from State Street?

A. February 10, 1896.

———◆———

Q. How did Mayor Swift cut expenses in January 1896?

A. He ordered 2,300 street lamps darkened.

Q. What Illinois political leader and U.S. senator from Illinois, nicknamed the Little Giant, achieved lasting national fame for his series of debates on the slavery issue in 1858?

A. Stephen Arnold Douglas (the Lincoln-Douglas debates).

Q. What Chicagoan won the Nobel Peace Prize in 1931?

A. Jane Addams.

Q. What did the Chicago Board of Election Commissioners vote to purchase in June 1911 despite opposition from one of the three-member board?

A. One thousand voting machines at a total cost of $942,500.

Q. Why did the largest crowd seen in Chicago since the World's Columbian Exposition flock to Grant Park on August 12, 1911?

A. To witness the largest aviation meet ever held in the United States.

Q. In 1911, WCTU members petitioned to have what principal of Chicago's Willard High School removed for saying, "A saloon-keeper . . . of good character . . . is as much entitled to respect as anyone"?

A. Grace Reed.

Q. When James W. ("Bet-a-Million") Gates died in Paris in 1911 at the age of 66, how much was his estate worth?

A. $38 million.

Q. When did the world's first juvenile court open?

A. The Juvenile Court of Cook County opened in 1899.

Q. Who led a Civil Rights march on the Chicago city hall in 1965?

A. The Reverend Martin Luther King, Jr.

———◆———

Q. Who was the first Union officer killed in the Civil War?

A. Col. Elmer E. Ellsworth, founder of the Chicago Zouaves, May 24, 1861.

———◆———

Q. Fifty years after the Civil War began, how many veterans marched in Chicago's Grand Army of the Republic parade on Memorial Day, 1911?

A. 1,740, with 213 riding.

———◆———

Q. What drew an estimated 200,000 spectators to the Loop September 27, 1919?

A. A biplane piloted by Walter Brookins, flying at 2,500 feet for twenty minutes.

———◆———

Q. How much did firewood sell for in Chicago in 1847?

A. A wagonload for four dollars.

———◆———

Q. Who betrayed John Dillinger to the FBI in 1934?

A. Anna Sage, the Lady in Red.

———◆———

Q. Because it had no tobacco, whiskey, beer, theaters, doctors, drugs, pork or oysters, in March 1911 Zion erected a sign at its corporate limits announcing it was what kind of city?

A. "Perfect."

Q. What did a group of Chicago businessmen do June 1, 1896, to protest the lack of street cleaning?

A. Swept North Avenue for several blocks and burned the mayor and several aldermen in effigy.

◆

Q. What agreement ended the International Harvester strike on May 6, 1916?

A. The workers won a minimum wage of twenty-five cents an hour plus time-and-a-half for overtime.

◆

Q. Why were regular workdays the best time in August 1910 to get one's shoes shined?

A. Chicago bootblacks charged five cents on weekdays but doubled the price for weekends and holidays.

◆

Q. Why did a municipal court judge in Chicago rule in 1911 that an auto livery firm did not have to carry black passengers?

A. Because the company was not a public operation.

◆

Q. What kinds of autos did the South Park board banish in the spring of 1902?

A. Steam, gasoline, or any car able to exceed eight miles an hour, as well as all whistles or horns.

◆

Q. What was former Governor Altgeld doing when he suffered a stroke at the Joliet Opera House in March 1902?

A. Speaking in behalf of the Boers.

◆

Q. In mid-May 1902 when evangelist Billy Sunday preached against playing golf on Sunday in Wheaton, what did Chicago Golf Club members do?

A. Teed off as usual.

Q. What happened to an attempt in 1824 to change the state's constitution to allow slavery?

A. It was defeated, although indentured workers were permitted until the Civil War.

Q. What brought Mother Jones, the eighty-three-year-old labor activist, to Chicago from New York in 1917?

A. The garment workers' strike.

Q. When was the first Illinois penitentiary opened?

A. In 1833, at Alton, with twenty-four cells.

Q. What was the Indian response during the 1833 treaty meeting in Chicago when told the "great Father in Washington" knew they wished to sell their land?

A. That the "great Father . . . had seen a bad bird, which had told him a lie."

Q. What founder of the Christian Catholic Apostolic church prophesied just before he died in Zion City in 1907 that he would return to earth in a thousand years?

A. John Alexander Dowie.

Q. How much did the Chicago stock market lose in 1907 during the biggest crash in years?

A. An average of five dollars per share.

Q. How much did Judge Kenesaw Mountain Landis of the U.S. district court fine the Standard Oil Company in 1907 for taking rebates from the Chicago and Alton Railroad?

A. $29,240,000, the largest fine on record.

Q. In what Illinois town did the Mormon leader Joseph Smith die?

A. Carthage, where he and his brother Hyrum were killed in 1844 by a mob while being held in jail.

———◆———

Q. Why did the first wife and widow of Mormon leader Joseph Smith remain in Nauvoo when most of his followers left for Utah in 1846?

A. She disliked polygamy and later married a non-Mormon.

———◆———

Q. What reception did Chicago give Eugene Debs when he was freed from the Woodstock jail November 22, 1895?

A. He was welcomed at Northwestern Station by 10,000 workmen.

———◆———

Q. What distinction did Ella Flagg Young achieve in Chicago in 1909?

A. She became the first woman to head the school system of any large city in the nation.

———◆———

Q. How much did Charles E. Merriam spend in his losing campaign for mayor of Chicago?

A. He reported in April 1911 that he had spent $133,454.

———◆———

Q. The Chicago *Daily News* sponsored a commemoration of what major event at a mass meeting in the Auditorium in 1911?

A. The fiftieth anniversary of the firing on Fort Sumter.

———◆———

Q. Why did the Cook County grand jury in 1904 vote a true bill against Walter S. Boyle, Jr.?

A. For breaking the state speed limit of 15 mph in an automobile.

Q. Who was one of the first women to manage her own store in Illinois?

A. May Ann ("Auntie") Gogin of Palestine.

———◆———

Q. What did Christmas trees cost in Chicago in 1904?

A. The price for a fair-sized tree was up from $1 to $1.50 over 1903, and the trees were not so good.

———◆———

Q. How many casualties resulted from a week-long race riot that broke out on a south side Chicago beach July 27, 1919?

A. There were 33 dead and 306 hurt, with 2,000 made homeless.

———◆———

Q. What did the Chicago board of education order 8,000 teachers to do or face dismissal September 1, 1915?

A. Resign from the Chicago Teachers' Federation.

———◆———

Q. According to the *Tribune* of September 3, 1915, how much of Chicago's land was owned by ten families?

A. More than one-twelfth, with the Marshall Field family's holdings valued at $100 million.

———◆———

Q. How many pedestrians were killed by Chicago motorists in August 1913?

A. Nine.

———◆———

Q. What did Chief John Campion tell fellow survivors of the Chicago Fire of 1871 at the tenth annual get-together in 1913?

A. "That stuff about the party and Mrs. O'Leary's cow is all bunk."

HISTORY

Q. Why did the Reverend Beverly Ellison Warner of New Orleans criticize the University of Chicago at its 1905 convocation?

A. For giving a degree to a black graduate.

------♦------

Q. In what year did Sears, Roebuck open its first retail store?

A. 1925 (in Chicago).

------♦------

Q. What festive announcement did the Pullman Company make just before Christmas, 1915?

A. On New Year's Day raises totaling $600,000 would go to conductors and porters.

------♦------

Q. Why did the gunboat *Nashville*, which saw service in the Spanish-American War, come to Chicago June 5, 1909?

A. To be training ship for the U.S. Naval Reserve.

------♦------

Q. When a woman bather was arrested in the summer of 1913 at Jackson Park for going into the lake in bloomers, what happened in court?

A. Her apparel was ruled legal and proper.

------♦------

Q. What Irish nationalist drew a full house and raised $10,000 at Chicago's Orchestra Hall in September 1908 for an Irish home rule rally?

A. John Redmond.

------♦------

Q. What warning about national foreign policy did Mayor Thompson issue in late March 1917?

A. That "hysteria" might lead the United States into war.

Q. Why did Chicago police try to break up a mass meeting in May 1917, which drew 4,000 to the Auditorium and another 2,000 overflow crowd?

A. Because Dean Robert Morss Lovett of the University of Chicago was addressing a peace rally.

———◆———

Q. What course did the Chicago school board vote 13 to 8 to drop in January 1916?

A. Instruction in sex hygiene, after a four-month trial.

———◆———

Q. How many Civil War generals were residents of Galena?

A. Nine: Grant, Rawlins, Chetlain, Parker, Rowley, John E. Smith, John S. Smith, Maltby, and Duer.

———◆———

Q. Where was Lincoln's famous "house divided" speech delivered?

A. In the former state capitol in Springfield.

———◆———

Q. The Civil War Round Table, which has chapters across the nation, was founded on what date?

A. December 3, 1940, by Ralph Newman, a Lincoln scholar from Chicago.

———◆———

Q. What was the Trail of Tears that passed through Illinois?

A. The forced march of 8,000 Cherokee Indians from four southern states during the winter of 1838-39 when many died.

———◆———

Q. The U.S. Senate voted, 55 to 28, on July 13, 1912, to expel what senator from Chicago for "buying" his seat?

A. William Lorimer.

Q. Only four Civil War veterans turned up on November 4, 1912, for what reunion?

A. Survivors of the Ellsworth Zouaves and the Lincoln Wide-Awakes.

———◆———

Q. In March 1908, why did the Chicago police department announce a policy of driving all anarchists from the city?

A. A recent immigrant from Russia had tried to assassinate the police chief.

———◆———

Q. What new Chicago regulation applied to the sale of milk in May 1908?

A. Open cans were forbidden, with bottles required.

———◆———

Q. How did James A. Patten and his associates make $500,000 to $750,000 on July 21, 1909?

A. By selling four million bushels of September and December wheat.

———◆———

Q. Why did Chicago bakeries drop the price of bread to five cents a loaf after trying for three weeks in June 1898 to sell it at six cents?

A. Housewives were not buying.

———◆———

Q. What happened to Emma Goldman, the Red Queen, as she was about to speak at Chicago's Workingmen's Hall March 6, 1908?

A. Police forced her off the stage.

———◆———

Q. What did Governor Dunne sign in 1913 that pleased a large segment of Illinoisans?

A. The bill giving Illinois women limited suffrage.

Q. How did President Harper of the University of Chicago respond to attacks on Dr. Hermann E. Von Holst for opposing the war with Spain?

A. He said: "Every professor of this university has the right to think as he pleases on any and all subjects."

———◆———

Q. When did France cede the Illinois area to the British?

A. 1763, under terms of the Treaty of Paris following the Seven Years' War.

———◆———

Q. Why did three thousand women brave a downpour to march to the Chicago Coliseum June 7, 1916?

A. To tell the Republican national convention they wanted full suffrage.

———◆———

Q. Who headed the board of Lady Managers of the World's Columbian Exposition in 1893?

A. Mrs. Potter Palmer, Chicago social leader.

———◆———

Q. On October 24, 1931, what befell Al Capone, who controlled the Chicago underworld?

A. An eleven-year sentence for income tax evasion.

———◆———

Q. What change in the composition of the Chicago Board of Education did Mayor Dunne make in 1905?

A. Appointed three women, including Jane Addams.

———◆———

Q. What Pekin-born powerful Republican senator from Illinois served as minority leader from 1959 until his death in 1969?

A. Everett M. Dirksen.

Q. What Jacksonville woman was one of the founders of the Daughters of the American Revolution in 1912?

A. Ellen Hardin Walworth.

———◆———

Q. What did the woman president of the Anti-Cigarette League do in 1909 when she spotted a fourteen-year-old boy smoking on a downtown Chicago street?

A. Had him arrested.

———◆———

Q. What Chicago-born-and-educated jurist was appointed by Pres. Gerald Ford to replace Justice William O. Douglas on the U.S. Supreme Court?

A. John P. Stevens.

———◆———

Q. Why was Chicago publisher Wilbur Storey horse-whipped on the street in 1870?

A. His paper called actresses in Chicago's first burlesque show "bawds."

———◆———

Q. Military training was instituted in Chicago high schools in the fall of what year?

A. 1916.

———◆———

Q. Why did Lake Forest residents in the fall of 1905 seek to close a dairy farm run by Mrs. Scott Durand "for the pleasure of it"?

A. They found flies and the mooing of cows unpleasant.

———◆———

Q. Why was Ellen Gates Starr of Hull House charged with disorderly conduct in 1914?

A. For picketing Henrici's restaurant.

Q. What happened in the early 1900s when Loop restaurant owners refused to pay waitresses eight dollars for a six-day week?

A. Eight hundred fifty waitresses went on strike.

◆

Q. What settlement was reached to end the milk strike in April 1916?

A. The dairies agreed to pay the farmer more but kept the retail price at eight cents a quart.

◆

Q. Why was the passport of Mary McDowell, a Chicagoan, delayed in 1918 when she was invited to visit the YWCA facilities abroad?

A. She was a suspected pacifist.

◆

Q. How did the Commercial Club and the B'nai B'rith plan to clean up Chicago in 1919?

A. By wiping out white slavery and prostitution.

◆

Q. How many Leap Year babies were born in Chicago February 29, 1896?

A. 100.

◆

Q. How many women graduated in the class of 1887 at Kent College of Law?

A. One, Virginia Dixon, in a class of eighty-four.

◆

Q. Although the promoters lost $50,000, why did they declare themselves satisfied with the result of the aviation meet held in Chicago in 1911?

A. Oscar A. Brindley, in a Wright biplane, set a world altitude mark of 11,726 feet.

Q. What happened to a bill proposed in 1911 by Rep. E. J. Murphy of Chicago that made it illegal for women to wear baggy pantaloons or a hobble-skirt less than fifty-four inches in circumference?

A. It died.

———◆———

Q. In 1902, how many Chicago families had seven or more children of school age?

A. 6,144.

———◆———

Q. What program designed to help Germany pay its World War I reparations was named for the Chicago banker who headed the international committee which designed it, for which he shared the Nobel Peace Prize in 1925?

A. The Dawes Plan, named for Charles G. Dawes.

———◆———

Q. Who was primarily responsible for an Illinois anti-slavery vote?

A. The state's second governor, Edward Coles.

———◆———

Q. What royal visitor stopped off in Chicago for a few hours in 1897?

A. Liliuokalani, former queen of the Sandwich, or Hawaiian, Islands.

———◆———

Q. Why did 100 friends of John T. McCutcheon, *Tribune* cartoonist and war correspondent, throw him a party in January 1916?

A. Because of his coming marriage to socialite Evelyn Shaw.

———◆———

Q. When was Northwestern University chartered?

A. 1851.

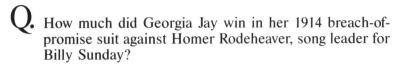

Q. How much did Georgia Jay win in her 1914 breach-of-promise suit against Homer Rodeheaver, song leader for Billy Sunday?

A. $20,000.

———◆———

Q. What did delegates to the 1914 convention of the General Federation of Women's Clubs protest?

A. New Paris fashions of slit skirts and tight gowns.

———◆———

Q. Why in 1912 did many prominent Chicago women say one could be young at any age?

A. Because the YWCA hotel said residents over twenty-five must move.

———◆———

Q. What Chicago financier was U.S. vice president under Calvin Coolidge?

A. Charles G. Dawes.

———◆———

Q. How much was Mrs. William McKinley's bill at Marshall Field's for ten changes of costume for her husband's inaugural ceremonies?

A. Between $8,000 and $10,000.

———◆———

Q. How did Mrs. Louise De Koven Bowen, president of the Chicago Juvenile Protective Association, refer to the city's dance halls in 1911?

A. As "training schools for vice."

———◆———

Q. During his first newspaper interview, who told *Tribune* reporter Genevieve Forbes Herrick, "The people want booze, and I sell 'em what they want"?

A. Al Capone.

HISTORY

Q. Why did WCTU members attack Mayor Harrison in 1898?

A. He permitted tobacco licenses to be reduced from $100 to $10.

———◆———

Q. What two famous African Americans became acquainted at Chicago's Quinn Chapel August 11, 1908?

A. Booker T. Washington and Jack Johnson.

———◆———

Q. Who approved bloomer-type swimsuits for thin women in 1914 but said they were "immoral, dangerous, and ridiculous" on fat women?

A. Chicago police chief Schuettler.

———◆———

Q. What position did Letitia Baldridge hold prior to becoming director of merchandising services at Chicago's Merchandise Mart?

A. Social secretary for Mrs. John F. Kennedy.

———◆———

Q. What sixty-five-year-old widow disappeared February 17, 1977, while on her way home from Rochester, Minnesota?

A. Helen Brach, whose late husband was president of the Brach Candy company.

———◆———

Q. How many people died when the excursion steamer *Eastland* capsized at her pier on July 24, 1915?

A. 812.

———◆———

Q. What drew five associate judges of the U.S. Supreme Court to Chicago on July 4, 1910?

A. Funeral services for the chief justice, Melville W. Fuller.

Q. In 1902, how did Charles S. Deneen utilize modern technology to win the campaign for governor?

A. He used his automobile to attend seventy-six meetings in sixteen days.

———◆———

Q. What did the nineteenth-century social activist and reformer Dorothea Dix protest about in the first state prison at Alton?

A. Insanitary conditions.

———◆———

Q. What was the name of Abraham Lincoln's stepmother, whom he visited just before leaving Illinois for the last time?

A. Sarah Bush Lincoln.

———◆———

Q. What was the circulation of the Chicago *Tribune* when it began publication in 1847?

A. 400.

———◆———

Q. In 1882, Jane Addams received one of the first bachelor's degrees conferred by what educational institution?

A. Rockford Female Seminary.

———◆———

Q. What top graduate of the Northwestern University law school later became secretary of labor and a justice of the U.S. Supreme Court?

A. Chicagoan Arthur Goldberg.

———◆———

Q. What unusual information was learned in 1911 about Pvt. Albert D. J. Cashier who served in the Civil War with the Ninety-fifth Illinois Volunteers?

A. That he was a woman, Jennie Hodgers, of Belvidere.

Q. How many were killed in one of the country's worst rail accidents near Chatsworth in 1887?

A. Eighty-five of the 500 passengers died when an excursion train of twenty wooden cars hit a blazing culvert.

———◆———

Q. Why did the Illinois legislature need to approve Myra Bradwell's becoming publisher of the highly successful *Legal News* in 1868?

A. Because it was illegal for a woman to operate a business at that time.

———◆———

Q. When did Illinois pass the country's first statewide law establishing payments from public funds to poor parents for the care of their children?

A. 1911.

———◆———

Q. What did the Peoria area celebrate in 1891?

A. Its tricentennial.

———◆———

Q. What did Moses Pettingill organize in 1842?

A. The Peoria Anti-Slavery Society.

———◆———

Q. What woman was seriously considered as a mayoral candidate in Chicago in 1923 but failed to get Republican party backing?

A. Louise De Koven Bowen, sixty-three-year-old treasurer of Hull House.

———◆———

Q. Why did Federal troops occupy Cairo ten days after the Fort Sumter attack starting the Civil War?

A. It had an important supply depot.

Q. Who was the target for the bombing in Chicago in October 1908?

A. Jim O'Leary, son of Catherine-of-the-Fire, who ran a gambling joint on North Halsted.

◆

Q. What factor was preventing "teacher after teacher" from taking jobs in Chicago, according to the superintendent of schools in 1908?

A. The fact that the top salary was $1,200 a year.

◆

Q. Why was Arthur Burrage Farwell refused admittance as an "improper person" to the brewers' convention at the Chicago Coliseum in 1911?

A. A "reformer," he planned to speak on the dangers of drink.

◆

Q. How many automobile traffic accidents were there in Chicago during the first five months of 1909?

A. 641 nonfatal and 31 fatal.

◆

Q. Who told the Civil Service commissioner on October 17, 1911, that there was no gambling in Chicago, that the police were honest, and there was no "open flaunting of vice"?

A. John McWeeny, chief of police.

◆

Q. Why did Charles C. Healey, Chicago chief of police for eighteen months, resign on December 11, 1916?

A. Mayor Thompson asked him to do so, and later he was arrested for extortion, bribery, and conspiracy.

◆

Q. What was the price of the *Daily Tribune* reduced to on October 3, 1910?

A. Two cents (Sunday papers still were a nickel).

Q. What city ordinance did Chicago mayor Swift refuse to veto in December 1896?

A. One establishing a four-cent streetcar fare

———◆———

Q. The Chicago Teachers Club and other groups met in February 1897 to protest the sale of what product?

A. Cigarettes, as they were "poison-laden, memory-destroying, and corrupting."

———◆———

Q. Why were fifteen barbers arrested at the Great Northern Hotel October 16, 1895?

A. For working on Sundays.

———◆———

Q. What happened to the 1895 law requiring barbershops in Illinois to close on Sundays?

A. It was declared unconstitutional.

———◆———

Q. What did Capt. Chelsey Blake of the steamer *Illinois* do when he discovered a fugitive slave aboard after leaving Chicago?

A. Made an unscheduled stop at a Canadian port and "furiously" ordered the stowaway off—into liberty.

———◆———

Q. What did the term "Long Nine" signify in relation to Illinois politics?

A. Lincoln and eight other legislators were tall for their time, their aggregate height reaching fifty-four feet.

———◆———

Q. How did Chicago teachers benefit the day before New Year's 1915?

A. The board of education boosted their pay $150 a year to $3,200.

Q. What happened in 1894 when George Pullman cut wages at his sleeping-car factory but failed to lower rents for the workers' housing?

A. The workers struck and were backed by the American Railway Union, headed by Eugene Debs.

———◆———

Q. How much did Chicago subscribe for the Liberty Loan drive in 1917?

A. 3.3 million, $70,000 over quota.

———◆———

Q. What caused the National Security League to cancel the membership of Mayor Thompson in August 1917?

A. He was not considered patriotic.

———◆———

Q. Why did horses pull the North Clark Street streetcars for a few hours on December 6, 1904?

A. A cable broke.

———◆———

Q. What were maximum police and firemen salaries after Mayor Busse approved a 10 percent raise in November 1910?

A. Policemen, $100 monthly; firemen, $103.75.

———◆———

Q. What Jacksonville native was the first woman ever chosen to represent the United States in another country, serving as U.S. minister to Denmark from 1933 to 1936?

A. Ruth Bryan Owens, eldest daughter of William Jennings Bryan.

———◆———

Q. What did Alderman F. W. Lipps urge Congress to do in January 1914?

A. Make it illegal for any auto to be capable of going more than 20 mph.

Q. What did the *Tribune* do on November 11, 1895?

A. Cut the daily paper price to one cent.

———◆———

Q. What major change did Chicago's volunteer fire department undergo in 1858?

A. It became professional.

———◆———

Q. In September 1908, what did the Chicago school board do to abolish high school fraternities?

A. Instructed principals to expel any student found belonging to one.

———◆———

Q. What effect did Prohibition, which began at midnight June 30, 1919, have on "Hinky Dink" Kenna's Workingmen's Exchange?

A. The First Ward saloon went dry one-half hour before the deadline because the beer ran out.

———◆———

Q. How did a presumably thirsty Polish novelist describe Chicago during a visit in July 1919?

A. Ladislaus St. Reymont said Chicago was ugly and Prohibition even worse.

———◆———

Q. What famous Sauk Indian chief was noted for his struggle against the westward movement of the white men in Illinois, his refusal to leave his Rock Island village in 1832 resulting in an American war called by his name?

A. Black Hawk.

———◆———

Q. What was the annual salary of Shadrach Bond, the first Illinois governor?

A. $1,000.

Q. Why did Richard J. Oglesby resign as governor only ten days after taking office for a second term in 1872?

A. He went into the U.S. Senate.

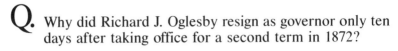

Q. What office did Richard J. Oglesby hold, beginning in 1884?

A. Governor for the third time.

Q. Eight Chicago police lieutenants admitted in March 1917 that they were promoted from sergeant through what illegal means?

A. By paying Chief Healey.

Q. How much did Chicago's first Tag Day on November 24, 1908, raise for children's charities?

A. $20,000.

Q. What did the arrest of eight members of the Illinois Athletic club for playing poker coincide with?

A. The inaugural address of the new club president, Robert H. McCormick, assistant U.S. district attorney.

Q. What committee was founded in 1919 as a result of the Chicago race riots?

A. The Race Commission.

Q. What threat did the Chicago City Collector make June 4, 1910, against motorists and teamsters?

A. All whose wheel taxes were unpaid within forty-eight hours would be barred from the streets.

Q. Why was a special Municipal Court established in Chicago on June 2, 1912?

A. To hear speeding charges against motorists.

———◆———

Q. Why did Chicago streetcar employees vote to strike in August 1909?

A. A wage increase was denied.

———◆———

Q. How could owners reclaim the seventy-three stray goats rounded up in 1910 in the Western and Chicago Avenue neighborhood?

A. By paying one dollar per goat.

———◆———

Q. Why were ten of Chicago's major packers indicted by a grand jury on September 12, 1910?

A. For alleged conspiracy in restraint of trade.

———◆———

Q. The police reported what crime record in November 1917?

A. The theft of thirty-three autos in forty-eight hours.

———◆———

Q. Who was mayor of Waukegan six times, three as a Democrat and three as a Republican?

A. Robert Sabonjian, former alderman and postmaster.

———◆———

Q. Who organized and financed the South Side Boys Club for Negroes in 1921?

A. Samuel Insull, the utilities magnate.

Q. When was the last time that Illinois voted for a Democrat in the presidential election?

A. 1964, for Lyndon B. Johnson.

———◆———

Q. What organizer of the Illinois abolitionist movement served as a pastor in Princeton for seventeen years and as a member of the U.S. House of Representatives?

A. Owen Lovejoy.

———◆———

Q. What did Illinoisan William Pinkerton do in the Civil War?

A. Headed the Union secret service.

———◆———

Q. What decision was an arbitration board considering in Chicago in September 1902?

A. How many times a day a mechanic could go out for a beer before being fired.

———◆———

Q. What caused over 100 people to become ill following a dinner for Archbishop George W. Mundelein at the University Club in Chicago February 10, 1916?

A. Arsenic put in the soup by an "anti-clerical fanatic."

———◆———

Q. What act of conscience ended former Illinois governor Altgeld's political career?

A. In 1892 he pardoned three still-imprisoned Haymarket Riot "anarchists."

———◆———

Q. Who said in August 1918 that sending former Chicago mayor William Hale Thompson to the U.S. Senate would be a disaster?

A. Former president Teddy Roosevelt.

Q. The timing for the two great world's fairs, the World's Columbian Exposition and the Century of Progress Exposition, had what in common?

A. Both took place during major national depressions, in 1893 (the Panic of 1893 which lasted until 1898) and in 1933-34 (the Great Depression, 1929-1939).

◆

Q. Before becoming president, thus commander-in-chief, Abraham Lincoln's only military experience had been that of a company officer in what minor war?

A. Black Hawk War, in 1832.

◆

Q. What did the thirty-three nurses of Michal Reese graduating class volunteer in 1918?

A. To serve as a group in France.

◆

Q. What French explorer traveled with La Salle through the Illinois region in 1680, then took charge of Fort St. Louis, a stronghold built at Starved Rock?

A. Henri de Tonti.

◆

Q. The last of the Lincoln-Douglas debates took place in what city?

A. Alton.

◆

Q. Why did a crowd of men and women cheer Emmeline Pankhurst at Orchestra Hall in 1909?

A. The British suffragette advocated votes for women.

◆

Q. Evelyn Echols, founder of the Echols Travel and Hotel Schools, is a member of what prestigious women's group?

A. The Committee of 200, composed of America's leading businesswomen.

Q. What vice president of the United States was an unsuccessful candidate for governor of Illinois, while his grandson with the same name was governor of Illinois but was unsuccessful in his bid for the vice presidency?

A. Adlai Ewing Stevenson.

———◆———

Q. Who killed Pontiac, the Indian chief who led Indian warriors along the frontier in 1763-1765?

A. A drunken Peoria Indian, in 1769.

———◆———

Q. One of the earliest known black American newspapers still in circulation, the *Chicago Defender* was founded by Robert S. Abbott in what year?

A. 1905.

———◆———

Q. Whom did the Chicago Press Club elect as president January 12, 1896?

A. Joseph Medill of the *Tribune*.

———◆———

Q. The momentous Dred Scott Decision was handed down by the U.S. Supreme Court in response to the suit filed by the black servant of a resident of what town?

A. Rock Island.

———◆———

Q. How much was the 1913 income tax of Julius Rosenwald, president of Sears, Roebuck?

A. More than anyone else in town: $1,320,000.

———◆———

Q. When was the first National Anti-Slavery reunion held?

A. June 10, 1874, at the Second Baptist Church of Chicago.

Q. What full-blooded Seneca Indian was an aspiring lawyer, a construction engineer, and a Civil War general?

A. Ely S. Parker, who was refused admittance to the bar because of his race.

Q. Who was Chicago's first female physician?

A. Dr. Mary Harris Thompson (1863).

Q. What high honor did fourteen-year-old Orion Howe, a Civil War drummer from Waukegan, receive during the war?

A. The Congressional Medal of Honor.

Q. What powerful Republican, a Danville resident, served in the U.S. House of Representatives for forty-six years and as speaker from 1903 to 1911, eventually causing the House to vote to limit the speaker's authority?

A. Joseph Gurney ("Uncle Joe") Cannon.

Q. How many Illinois men were killed in the Civil War?

A. Approximately 37,000.

Q. What former University of Chicago economics professor, later a leading liberal Democratic U.S. senator from Illinois, helped revise the Federal Social Security Act in 1939?

A. Paul Howard Douglas.

Q. Dan Rostenkowski, chairman of the Ways and Means Committee since 1981, was born in what Illinois city?

A. Chicago.

Q. What World War II naval veteran became president of Bell and Howell at age twenty-nine, then defeated his former University of Chicago economics professor in a race for the U.S. Senate?

A. Charles H. Percy.

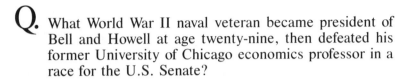

Q. What Salem-born graduate of Illinois College and the University of Chicago was an unsuccessful vice-presidential candidate in 1924 but later twice governor of Nebraska?

A. Charles Wayland Bryan, brother of Williams Jennings Bryan.

Q. How many names are on the Illinois Vietnam Veterans Memorial in Springfield's Oakridge Cemetery?

A. 2,967, the total of the state's dead and missing.

Q. In what year did French explorer Pere Marquette first travel the Illinois River?

A. 1673.

Q. The first statue honoring a black Illinois citizen in the state capitol building in Springfield is of what legislator nationally known for his work on the Race Commission?

A. Adelbert H. Roberts.

Q. What pledge did Mayor Harrison make September 1, 1897?

A. To clean up Chicago streets and "garbage-laden alleys."

ARTS & LITERATURE

CHAPTER FOUR

Q. What British poet wrote, in 1886, that "the most intelligent and thoughtful criticism" of his work came from Chicago literary societies?

A. Robert Browning.

———◆———

Q. When Al Capone refused to provide material "unfair to my people," what Chicago *Daily News* columnist gave up the idea of writing his biography?

A. Howard Vincent O'Brien.

———◆———

Q. What Chicagoan was the world authority on Sherlock Holmes and a co-founder of the Baker Street Irregulars?

A. Vincent Starrett.

———◆———

Q. Who wrote *The Disinherited*, an early proletarian novel?

A. Jack Conroy, a migratory worker who became a Chicago literary figure.

———◆———

Q. What did the Chicago *Tribune* present to the Truman library in 1973?

A. A bronze replica of the 1948 front page headlined Dewey Beats Truman.

Q. What poet, song-writer, and author of children's books, sold hot dogs at White Sox games to help pay tuition at the Art Institute?

A. Cartoonist and illustrator Shel Silverstein.

———◆———

Q. Robert Lewis Taylor, Illinois-born novelist and journalist, wrote what book about the life of suffragette Carrie Nation?

A. *Vessel of Wrath.*

———◆———

Q. After visiting Chicago briefly in 1911, what British author called it "ugly but immense"?

A. Arnold Bennett.

———◆———

Q. When asked to send one of his portraits to Chicago in 1896, what American painter replied, "Send one of my masterpieces to such a place as Chicago? Never!"?

A. James A. M. Whistler, then living in England.

———◆———

Q. When the new Winnetka Public Library opened September 1, 1910, for whom was it named?

A. Henry Demarest Lloyd, whose four sons donated the building.

———◆———

Q. The museum at Bishop Hill contains an outstanding collection of Early American primitive paintings by what foremost American folk artist?

A. Olof Krans.

———◆———

Q. What college town is the home of twenty-four religious publishers and organizations, as well as the Billy Graham Center devoted to Christian evangelism?

A. Wheaton.

Q. In the early 1920s, what two books did New York-born author Ben Hecht write about life in Chicago following World War I?

A. *1001 Afternoons in Chicago* and *Tales of Chicago*.

——◆——

Q. What circulation did the Chicago Public Library claim in 1896?

A. The world's greatest for such an institution.

——◆——

Q. What novelist, born in Oak Park, received the 1954 Nobel Prize for literature?

A. Ernest Hemingway, with *The Old Man and the Sea*.

——◆——

Q. What Chicago-born journalist became famous for a series of books, all titled with the beginning word *Inside*, that drew on his observations as a foreign correspondent for the Chicago *Daily News*?

A. John Gunther.

——◆——

Q. Who wrote *The Front Page*, a rollicking stage play about Chicago police reporters?

A. Ben Hecht and Charles MacArthur.

——◆——

Q. What Chicago *Daily News* staffer won the Pulitzer Prize for editorial cartooning in 1969?

A. John Fischetti.

——◆——

Q. How was Benjamin Franklin's birthday observed in Chicago in 1910?

A. A group of printers held a dinner-dance at the LaSalle Hotel.

Q. What reformer, who was also a governor of Illinois, wrote the book *Our Penal Machinery and Its Victims* in 1884 which criticized the U.S. court system for discriminating against the poor?

A. John Peter Altgeld.

Q. What major poet, historian, and biographer was born in Galesburg and won a Pulitzer Prize for poetry in 1951 and Pulitzer Prize for history in 1940?

A. Carl Sandburg.

Q. Who designed Chicago's Home Insurance building, the world's first skyscraper supported by a steel skeleton?

A. William Le Barron Jenney, in 1884.

Q. What post did Daniel J. Terra of Kenilworth hold during the Reagan administration?

A. Ambassador-at-large for cultural affairs.

Q. How many persons attended the opening of the new Chicago Public Library building in September 1897?

A. More than ten thousand.

Q. What New York City writer hung the "Second City" tag on Chicago?

A. A. J. Leibling, husband of novelist Jean Stafford.

Q. What Wisconsin-born playwright, author of Pulitzer Prize-winning *Our Town*, was an English professor at the University of Chicago from 1930 to 1936?

A. Thornton Wilder.

Q. What Chicago native wrote *Nowhere City* in 1965?

A. Alison Lurie.

———◆———

Q. What Chicago-born left-wing author reversed course after writing such novels as *U.S.A.* and *Manhattan Transfer*?

A. John Dos Passos, who "ran out of dreams."

———◆———

Q. What best-seller did Bill Veeck and sportswriter Ed Linn create in 1962?

A. The lively *Veeck as in Wreck*.

———◆———

Q. What novelist is best known for describing the brutal life of the Chicago slums of the 1930s and 1940s, in such fiction as *The Man With the Golden Arm*?

A. Nelson Algren.

———◆———

Q. What Hope native and University of Illinois graduate was a distinguished writer, critic, and professor who won the Pulitzer Prize in poetry in 1940?

A. Mark Van Doren.

———◆———

Q. What major American architect working in Chicago in the late 1800s popularized the phrase "form follows function"?

A. Louis Sullivan.

———◆———

Q. What crusading editor and publisher made the Chicago *Tribune* one of the world's most successful newspapers during his tenure from 1855 until his death in 1874?

A. Joseph Medill.

Q. What music critic, novelist, and amateur photographer was fired from the Chicago *American* for "lowering the tone of the paper"?

A. Carl Van Vechten.

———◆———

Q. What literature-lover expanded the bookstore founded by his father into a Chicago-area chain?

A. Carl Kroch, of Kroch's & Brentano's.

———◆———

Q. What Chicago-born author who wrote *The Old Bunch*, a story about children of Russian-Jewish immigrants in Chicago, died in his home in Israel?

A. Meyer Levin.

———◆———

Q. The name of what Chicago-based publishing company is synonymous with atlases?

A. Rand McNally & Company.

———◆———

Q. What literate and readable columnist for the Chicago *Daily News* once described the job of disk-jockey as "Picking out the good records and playing the bad ones"?

A. Sydney Justin Harris.

———◆———

Q. What Jacksonville native won the National Book Award for his first novel, *Morte d'Urban*, in 1963?

A. J. F. Powers.

———◆———

Q. What controversial *Tribune* columnist is one of the nation's best known?

A. Mike Royko.

ARTS & LITERATURE

Q. What book by long-time Chicago newsman Don Russell won the coveted Western Writers of America Spur Award in 1961?

A. *Lives and Legends of Buffalo Bill.*

———◆———

Q. Archie, the typewriting cockroach, was the creation of what Walnut native?

A. Don Marquis.

———◆———

Q. What poet, a native of Glencoe, served as librarian of Congress and assistant secretary of state?

A. Archibald MacLeish.

———◆———

Q. What trilogy of novels by a Chicagoan explores the impact of industrial life on a boy growing up in a poor Chicago neighborhood?

A. The Studs Lonigan series by James T. Farrell.

———◆———

Q. What Waukegan native wrote the science-fiction masterpiece *The Martian Chronicles*?

A. Ray Bradbury.

———◆———

Q. To whom did the Chicago *Sun-Times* give their Book of the Year Award in 1990?

A. Richard Stern, for *Noble Rot*.

———◆———

Q. What Peoria native wrote *The Feminine Mystique* and later founded the National Organization for Women (NOW)?

A. Betty Friedan.

Q. Who now heads the firm of Rand McNally & Company?

A. Andrew McNally IV.

———◆———

Q. Kenan Heise, a *Tribune* staffer and authority on Chicago history, runs what Evanston bookstore?

A. The Chicago Historical Bookworks.

———◆———

Q. What was the real name of the Winnetka author who used the pseudonym Patrick Dennis when writing of his wildly lovable character Auntie Mame?

A. Everett Tanner III.

———◆———

Q. Who won the Polk Award in Journalism in 1990 for medical reporting?

A. John M. Crewdson of the Chicago *Tribune*.

———◆———

Q. *Guard of Honor* won a Pulitzer Prize in fiction in 1949 for what Chicago-born author?

A. James Gould Cozzens.

———◆———

Q. A statue of what native American by Lorado Taft was unveiled in July 1940 at Eagle's Nest, near Oregon, on the Rock River?

A. Chief Black Hawk.

———◆———

Q. What New York publisher and Lake Forest native re-issues the best out-of-print volumes on golf under the title, *Classics of Golf*?

A. Robert McDonald.

Q. Irving Wallace, author of *The Prize* and *The Miracle* among others, was born in what city?

A. Chicago.

———◆———

Q. What juvenile books did the Chicago city librarian order off the shelves in March 1911?

A. Titles by Horatio Alger, Jr., and Oliver Optic.

———◆———

Q. "Little Boy Blue" is perhaps the most famous poem of what former Chicago *Daily News* columnist who is known as the Poet of Childhood?

A. Eugene Field.

———◆———

Q. How was the Chicago Symphony Orchestra's centennial gala concert enlivened October 18, 1991?

A. Souvenir alarm clocks presented to patrons went off during the program.

———◆———

Q. What Chicago playwright won the Pulitzer Prize in drama in 1984 for his play *Glengarry Glen Ross*?

A. David Mamet.

———◆———

Q. Who played the title role in *Villon the Vagabond* at Chicago's Grand Opera House in September 1895?

A. Otis Skinner, who also produced it.

———◆———

Q. What Kenilworth resident created the Terra Museum on Chicago's Magnificent Mile?

A. Daniel J. Terra, an art collector for half a century.

Q. What is the title of the collection of stories, penned by Chicagoan Henry Blake Fuller, about Chicago artist life?

A. *Under the Skylights* (1901).

◆

Q. Dempster McMurphy, an employee of the *Daily News* promotion department, annually wrote a piece about what character who "roams the outfields of Eternity, making shoestring catches of lost souls"?

A. Dismas, the Good Thief.

◆

Q. What catapulted the Chicago Art Institute into the category of important museums?

A. The gift by Martin A. Ryerson of a group of Old Master paintings bought at auction for $200,000.

◆

Q. How much did John McCormack, the Irish tenor, pay for the manuscript of Eugene Field's "Little Boy Blue" at a charity bazaar in 1917?

A. $2,400.

◆

Q. The story of a poor girl alone in Chicago, partly based on the experiences of one of his sisters, *Sister Carrie* was the first novel of what major American writer?

A. Theodore Dreiser.

◆

Q. Why did the Chicago Grand Opera cancel its 1914-15 season?

A. Too many European singers were unavailable because of World War I.

◆

Q. What musical treat did Chicagoans have in January 1915?

A. Pablo Casals played the violin cello with the Chicago Symphony Orchestra.

Q. What attendance figure broke the record at the Ravinia Music Festival in Highland Park when *Lucia di Lammermoor* opened the season on July 1, 1956?

A. Seven thousand.

———◆———

Q. The Poetry Society prize of five hundred dollars for the best volume of poetry published in 1918 was divided between what two poets?

A. Margaret Widdemer for *The Old Road to Paradise* and Carl Sandburg for *Cornhusker*.

———◆———

Q. What theatrical group was formed by Nora Brooks Blakely, daughter of Gwendolyn Brooks?

A. The Chocolate Chips Theater Company in Chicago.

———◆———

Q. Approximately how many theaters are there in Chicago or within fifty miles of it?

A. 150 (the League of Chicago Theatres has 125 members).

———◆———

Q. Who founded Chicago's Ebony Museum, now the DuSable Museum of African American History, in 1961?

A. Margaret Burroughs.

———◆———

Q. How many guests attended the Seventh Annual Reception of the Chicago Art Institute in October 1895?

A. About 2,700.

———◆———

Q. On what occasion was William Jennings Bryan the keynote speaker before a capacity-plus crowd at Orchestra Hall in 1911?

A. The 300th anniversary of the issuance of the King James Bible.

Q. Why did Frederick Stock conduct the Chicago Symphony Orchestra on December 12, 1905, instead of Theodore Thomas, who had never missed conducting it in half a century?

A. The sixty-nine-year-old Thomas was on his death bed.

———◆———

Q. When John M. Wing, Chicago newspaperman, died in 1917, what bequest did he leave the Newberry Library?

A. $200,000 to purchase materials on printing.

———◆———

Q. Why did poets Carl Sandburg and Vachel Lindsay attend a Cliff Dwellers' dinner March 1, 1914?

A. To honor William Butler Yeats, the Irish poet.

———◆———

Q. What Victor Herbert operetta was performed in Chicago for the first time on March 28, 1914?

A. *Babette*, starring Fritzi Scheff.

———◆———

Q. What was odd about the fact that the University of Chicago Library reported in 1899 that 1,500 books had been stolen or were long overdue?

A. Most of them concerned theology.

———◆———

Q. What novel was one of the best-sellers in 1898 in Chicago?

A. *David Harum*, by David Noyes Westcott.

———◆———

Q. From 1913 to 1919, what sports reporter and author of humorous short stories wrote a column in the Chicago *Tribune* called "In the Wake of the News"?

A. Ringgold Wilmer ("Ring") Lardner.

Q. Chicago resident Richard Wright wrote what novel that deals with one day in the life of a black postal worker in Chicago?

A. *Lawd Today*.

Q. What novel by Chicago native Michael Crichton hit number one on the *Publisher's Weekly* bestseller list for fiction on February 17, 1992?

A. *Rising Sun*.

Q. Poet Edgar Lee Masters was law partner of what famous Chicago criminal lawyer?

A. Clarence Darrow.

Q. What Chicago realtor wrote *An Autobiography of Black Jazz*?

A. Dempsey Travis, who had his own band when he was sixteen.

Q. What Chicago-born newspaper publisher and editor helped influence the development of American journalism after buying the failing *Daily News* in 1876 and making it a successful, widely respected newspaper?

A. Victor Fremont Lawson.

Q. What rule did a Chicago library director wish to institute in December 1904?

A. That all patrons wash their hands before using books.

Q. What wage increase did the Actors and Chorus Union achieve in August 1907?

A. 15 percent (experienced chorus men now earned fifteen dollars weekly, ladies twelve dollars).

Q. From what organization did the Art Institute evolve?

A. The Chicago Academy of Design, founded in 1866.

———◆———

Q. *Spoon River Anthology* was the poetry masterpiece of what Kansas-born lawyer in Chicago?

A. Edgar Lee Masters.

———◆———

Q. What Chicago novelist wrote *The Bright Land*, a story of a nineteenth-century woman on the Illinois frontier?

A. Janet Ayer Fairbank.

———◆———

Q. What former *Tribune* reporter-turned-author was well known for his novel *The Voice of Bugle Ann* long before he won the Pulitzer Prize for his work describing the horrors of a Civil War Confederate prison camp?

A. MacKinley Kantor.

———◆———

Q. Now part of Lowden Memorial State Park near Oregon, what was the name of the colony of artists and writers during the first part of the century that included Lorado Taft and Hamlin Garland?

A. Eagle's Nest.

———◆———

Q. What happened when Mahalia Jackson, the great gospel singer, moved into a white neighborhood on South Indiana in 1956?

A. Threatening phone calls and a broken picture window.

———◆———

Q. When did Ludwig Mies Van der Rohe, the renowned architect, arrive in Chicago from Germany?

A. In 1938, one of many who preferred a free environment.

Q. What magazine, founded in Chicago in 1912 by poet Harriet Monroe, helped initiate and develop modern American poetry?

A. *Poetry: A Magazine of Verse.*

————◆————

Q. Although known as "the vagabond poet," what author of "The Congo" and "General William Booth Enters Into Heaven" was born and died in the same house in Springfield?

A. Vachel Lindsay.

————◆————

Q. What black artist, never fully recognized in his lifetime, was given a retrospective showing at the Chicago Historical Society in October 1991?

A. Archibald J. Motley, Jr.

————◆————

Q. Who created Mr. Dooley, a favorite Chicago philosopher, one of whose sayings was: " Trust everybody; but cut the cards!"?

A. Finley Peter Dunne.

————◆————

Q. What novel by Frank Harris involves the Haymarket Riot in Chicago?

A. *The Bomb.*

————◆————

Q. What four-volume work on Abraham Lincoln has 150,000 more words than all of Shakespeare's plays?

A. *The War Years*, by Galesburg-native Carl Sandburg, which won a Pulitzer Prize.

————◆————

Q. Who was the head of the first library school in the Midwest?

A. Katharine Sharp, later head librarian at the University of Illinois.

Q. The 1895 opera season in Chicago opened with what performance on November 18 with Walter Damrosch conducting?

A. *Tristan and Isolde.*

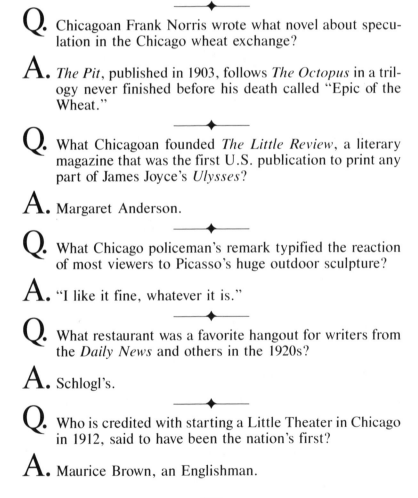

Q. What native of Mundelein who now lives in Alaska wrote *Edges of the Earth* in 1991?

A. Rick Leo.

Q. Chicagoan Frank Norris wrote what novel about speculation in the Chicago wheat exchange?

A. *The Pit,* published in 1903, follows *The Octopus* in a trilogy never finished before his death called "Epic of the Wheat."

Q. What Chicagoan founded *The Little Review,* a literary magazine that was the first U.S. publication to print any part of James Joyce's *Ulysses*?

A. Margaret Anderson.

Q. What Chicago policeman's remark typified the reaction of most viewers to Picasso's huge outdoor sculpture?

A. "I like it fine, whatever it is."

Q. What restaurant was a favorite hangout for writers from the *Daily News* and others in the 1920s?

A. Schlogl's.

Q. Who is credited with starting a Little Theater in Chicago in 1912, said to have been the nation's first?

A. Maurice Brown, an Englishman.

Q. Jack McPhaul, long-time Chicago newspaperman, wrote what book about the Windy City press?

A. *Deadlines & Monkeyshines*, in 1962.

◆

Q. Listed in the "Loop Sculpture Guide," issued by the Chicago Office of Fine Arts, "Batcolumn" by Claes Oldenburg depicts what object?

A. A 100-foot high baseball bat.

◆

Q. What did Mrs. Rose Fay Thomas present to the Newberry Library in October 1908?

A. All the orchestra scores used by her late husband, Theodore Thomas, during his career which included directing the Chicago Symphony Orchestra.

◆

Q. What executive editor of Chicago-based *Ebony* magazine is a recognized authority on black history, with nine books to his credit?

A. Lerone Bennett.

◆

Q. The Old Town School of Folk Music, offering classes ranging from guitar and piano to violin and harmonica, was founded in what year?

A. 1957.

◆

Q. Of whom was it said, "He made more hearts merry than any man who ever lived in Chicago"?

A. The Frenchman Mark Beaubien, hotel-keeper and fiddler, who arrived in 1826.

◆

Q. What happened to Crosby's Opera House, scheduled to open October 8, 1871, after a $100,000 remodeling?

A. The Great Chicago Fire remodeled it again.

Q. What *Tribune* column did Bert Leston Taylor write under the initials BLT?

A. "A Line o' Type or Two."

———◆———

Q. What is unusual about the Stations of the Cross in St. Patrick's Catholic Church near Lake Forest?

A. Artist Franklin McMahon, a parishioner, created the stations in ceramic tile; his wife, Irene, wrote the text, after visiting Jerusalem.

———◆———

Q. What three Chicagoans were the "Chicago Press Veterans of 1991"?

A. The Agrella brothers: Joe, Don, and Chris.

———◆———

Q. What distinction does the *Illinois Monthly Magazine* hold?

A. Begun in 1830 in Vandalia, it was the first literary periodical west of the Ohio.

———◆———

Q. What caused a near-panic during an opera performance at the Auditorium in November 1917?

A. A "home-made" bomb in the aisle, which failed to explode.

———◆———

Q. What press representative and media consultant for Chicago's Lyric Opera wrote a very popular "how to" book, *Subscribe Now*, giving tips on raising money for the performing arts?

A. Danny Newman.

———◆———

Q. What soprano, who created the role of Melisande in Claude Debussy's opera *Pelleas et Melisande*, studied voice in Chicago and later joined the Chicago Grand Opera Company?

A. Mary Garden (1874-1967).

Q. What *Tribune* police reporter was the first woman to be assigned to the press room of the Chicago Police Department's detective bureau?

A. Patricia (Pat) Leeds.

Q. What Highland Park resident founded *Other Voices*, a literary magazine which earned twelve Illinois Arts Council awards in its first three years?

A. Dolores Weinberg.

Q. Carol Spelius, a Deerfield poet/housewife, founded what publishing enterprise?

A. Lake Shore Publishing, with sixteen volumes of poetry and short stories now in print.

Q. What political office did William Benton, former University of Chicago vice president and publisher of the *Encyclopedia Britannica*, hold?

A. Senator from Connecticut.

Q. What 1964 book by John W. Allen offers a wealth of hard-to-find information?

A. *Legends & Lore of Southern Illinois.*

Q. Who began collecting daguerreotypes on Chicago's Maxwell Street as a youngster and has become one of the most knowledgeable dealers in photographics in the nation?

A. Clifford Krainik, of Graphic Antiquities, Falls Church, Virginia.

Q. Who joined the Chicago *Tribune* staff February 28, 1917?

A. Carey Orr, an editorial cartoonist.

Q. What contribution did music-lover Elizabeth Sprague Coolidge make to the Chicago Symphony in 1916?

A. $100,000 to the pension fund.

———◆———

Q. What former international editor for Chicago-published *Ebony* wrote *Native Daughter*, an autobiographical account of a black girl growing up in Driscoll, North Dakota?

A. Era Bell Thompson.

———◆———

Q. What wife of a chancellor of the University of Chicago wrote *These Ruins Are Inhabited* about life in England?

A. Muriel Beadle.

———◆———

Q. What Bloomington-born type designer and printer made 122 designs for type faces over a fifty-year period and received the gold medal of the American Institute of Graphic Arts?

A. Frederic William Goudy.

———◆———

Q. What former Chicagoan wrote *Cissy Patterson*, a biography of her great-aunt?

A. Alice Albright Hoge.

———◆———

Q. Who founded Ragdale in Lake Forest, said to be the only writers' colony in the Midwest?

A. Alice Ryerson Hayes, in 1976.

———◆———

Q. What former Quiz Kid, now a writer about gifted children and other educational topics, lives in Highland Park?

A. Ruth Duskin Feldman.

Q. What poet, who grew up in the Chicago community called "Bronzeville," won the first Pulitzer Prize ever given a black writer?

A. Gwendolyn Brooks, for *Annie Allen* in 1950.

Q. The popular *New Yorker* cartoonist Helen Hokinson was born in what Illinois town?

A. Mendota.

Q. What was the largest braille printing project in history, completed in 1961?

A. Translation of the *World Book Encyclopedia*, a project of Chicago-based Field Enterprises Educational Corporation (now World Book-Childcraft International, Inc.).

Q. What Highland Park resident wrote *Chicago Girls*, a best-selling novel of the late 1980s?

A. Edith Freund.

Q. What was the real name of Craig Rice, the Chicago-based mystery author and ghostwriter for Gypsy Rose Lee and George Sanders?

A. Georgiana Ann Randolph.

Q. What University of Chicago history professor wrote the three-volume *A History of Chicago*, now considered a classic?

A. Bessie Louise Pierce.

Q. India Moffett, former society editor for the Chicago *Tribune*, was appointed to what political post?

A. Assistant national committeewoman for the Democratic party.

Q. Why did women students at Northwestern University refuse to appear in Sheridan's *The Rivals* in 1902?

A. The play contains the word *damn*.

———◆———

Q. What American evangelist founded in Chicago a church, a Bible institute, and a press that operates a radio network, publishes books and magazines, and produces films?

A. Dwight L. Moody.

———◆———

Q. Maude Adams starred in a 1916 revival of *The Little Minister* at what Chicago theater?

A. The Blackstone.

———◆———

Q. What abolitionist clergyman and editor published the *Alton Observer* and helped organize the Illinois Anti-Slavery Society?

A. Elijah Lovejoy.

———◆———

Q. When was Caroline McIlvaine librarian of the Chicago Historical Society?

A. 1901 to 1926.

———◆———

Q. Who was literary editor of the *Tribune* for more than forty years?

A. Fanny Butcher, who died at ninety-nine.

———◆———

Q. What was the title of *Tribune* literary editor Fanny Butcher's 1972 autobiography?

A. *Many Lives—One Love.*

Q. What Wilmette resident learned to swim at age sixty, taught retarded youngsters to swim, and helped the Boy Scouts raise $60,000 for leader dogs?

A. Ben Kartman, newspaperman, magazine editor, president of Midland Authors, and journalism teacher.

———◆———

Q. What did supporters of the Theodore Thomas Orchestra accomplish by a dinner at Orchestra Hall in Chicago in March 1910?

A. Guests pledged $85,000 to help meet the orchestra's debt of $350,000.

———◆———

Q. Why were so many streetcar riders wearing tuxedos after Caruso's first Chicago appearance in April 1910?

A. There was a taxi driver strike—beginning one hour before the concert ended.

———◆———

Q. What native Chicagoan became artist-in-residence at the University of Wisconsin in 1948?

A. Aaron Bohrod, a WWII war artist.

———◆———

Q. Why did *Tribune* publisher Robert R. McCormick veto a book section at one time?

A. He is supposed to have said, "Readers of the *Tribune* don't read books."

———◆———

Q. After the Great Fire, what gift did Queen Victoria make to Chicago?

A. Books to help restock the public library.

———◆———

Q. Who designed the Women's Building at the Columbian Exposition after a competition among women architects?

A. Sophia Hayden of Boston.

Q. What author of the play *Mary, Mary* and of the book of humorous essays *Please Don't Eat the Daisies* attended Catholic University?

A. Jean Kerr.

Q. How many square feet are in the Harold Washington main library in downtown Chicago, which opened in 1991 as the world's largest?

A. 757,000.

Q. What entrepreneur founded and published *Ebony* and other magazines after borrowing $600 from his mother in 1942?

A. John Harold Johnson.

Q. When and by whom was the Midland Authors founded?

A. 1915 (charter members included Edna Ferber and Hamlin Garland, who became the first president).

Q. Who is the dean of Chicagoland's rare book dealers?

A. Richard S. Barnes, whose fourth bookshop in fifty-one years is in Evanston.

Q. Although the Ravinia Music Festival got the blues when it rained so often during the 1990 season that a $241,000 deficit resulted, what happened the next season?

A. A friendly drought insured a surplus of $184,000.

Q. Daniel Burnham's will left $50,000 to the Art Institute in 1912 for what purpose?

A. An architectural library.

Q. How many "private" seats are available at the new Harold Washington Library Center?

A. 2,200.

———◆———

Q. In 1991, what donor gave the Art Institute of Chicago its most valuable gift in forty-five years, a $50 million collection of seventy-seven surrealist works of art?

A. Lindy Bergman.

———◆———

Q. For the first time in its over 200-year history, what publisher began a retail venture in 1991 at Woodfield Mall in Schaumberg?

A. *The Encyclopedia Britannica.*

———◆———

Q. What 1989 graduate of the University of Illinois is the author of *Feminist Fatale*, a study of the women's movement past, present, and future?

A. Paula Kamen, a former reporter for the *Daily Illini.*

———◆———

Q. What Chicagoan wrote the children's book *There's No Such Thing as a Channuka Bush, Sandy Goldstein?*

A. Susan Sussman.

———◆———

Q. When the *Nutcracker* ballet, sponsored by the Chicago *Tribune*, was performed in December 1991, what director and choreographer was absent for the first time in twenty-four years?

A. Ruth Page, who had died the previous April.

———◆———

Q. What editor was responsible for removing the slogan "The World's Greatest Newspaper" from the Chicago *Tribune* masthead on January 1, 1977?

A. Clayton Kirkpatrick.

Q. What was the first theater in Chicago in which black patrons could sit wherever they chose?

A. The Peking Temple of Music at 2700 South State Street, which opened June 18, 1905.

------◆------

Q. Margaret Ayer Barnes wrote what 1930 Pulitzer Prize-winning novel about a Chicago matron in the jazz age?

A. *Years of Grace.*

------◆------

Q. How did the Chicago Symphony Orchestra association stimulate interest in 1914?

A. With a series of popular concerts at prices from 15 to 75 cents.

------◆------

Q. What Robinson native won the National Book Award in 1951 for his first novel, *From Here to Eternity*, which sold more than four million copies?

A. James Jones.

------◆------

Q. What play by James M. Barrie was a smash hit in its first Chicago showing in March 1899?

A. *The Little Minister.*

------◆------

Q. Who wrote *Trumbull Park*, a first-hand account of a black man moving into a hostile white neighborhood?

A. Frank London Brown.

------◆------

Q. *Fabulous Chicago*, an enlarged edition of which appeared in 1981, was written by whom?

A. The late Emmett Dedmon, executive editor of the Chicago *Sun-Times*.

Q. What American poet voiced this complaint in 1880: "Chicago sounds rough to the maker of verse;/ One comfort we have—Cincinnati sounds worse"?

A. Oliver Wendell Holmes, addressing the Chicago Commercial Club.

———◆———

Q. What author performed May 14, 1990, for the first time in his career, to benefit Northwestern University's *Tri-Quarterly* magazine?

A. Reynolds Price, award-winning novelist.

———◆———

Q. Who was Wesley Raymond Brinke of Edwardsville?

A. The nineteenth-century publisher of about three dozen books on Illinois counties.

———◆———

Q. What is unique about the University of Chicago Press?

A. It was the first of its kind in the United States.

———◆———

Q. What photography teacher at the Illinois Institute of Technology has been photographing Chicago's hot-dog stands since 1986 because she feels they are one of the few mom-and-pop businesses left?

A. Patty Carroll.

———◆———

Q. When was the Art Institute of Chicago founded?

A. May 9, 1879, at a meeting of civic leaders.

———◆———

Q. Who was the noted English journalist who wrote *If Christ Came to Chicago,* a work that examined the corruptions of the city?

A. William T. Stead.

Q. What Southern Illinois University professor was named Illinois Author of the Year for 1989-90 by the Illinois Association of Teachers of English?

A. Eugene B. Redmond.

Q. Eugene R. Kupjack of Park Ridge, who held patents on thirteen orthopedic devices, is world-famous for making what exhibits at the Art Institute of Chicago?

A. Miniature rooms, handmade to the smallest detail, in the Mrs. James Ward Thorne Collection.

Q. Crabbe Evers is the pseudonym for what authors of a series of mysteries centered around major league baseball?

A. Bill Brashler and Reinder Van Til.

Q. Who published and edited *Notes for the Curious*, a John Dickson Carr memorial journal?

A. The late Larry L. French, general counsel for Southern Illinois University.

Q. What Pulitzer prize-winning poet became the editor of *Poetry* magazine in the late 1930s?

A. George Dillon, author of *The Flowering Stone*.

Q. What history professor at Northwestern University wrote the noted biography *Henry VIII: The Mask of Royalty*?

A. Lacey Baldwin Smith.

Q. In 1976, what author, who moved to Chicago from Montreal when he was nine years old, received both the Nobel Prize for literature and the Pulitzer Prize for fiction?

A. Saul Bellow.

Q. What Hope native and University of Illinois graduate won the Pulitzer Prize in biography in 1939, the year before his brother won the prize in poetry?

A. Carl Van Doren.

Q. What novel by Chicago-born Jack Gelber relates the life of the Beat generation?

A. *On Ice*.

Q. What future New York drama critic met his wife when she was his student at Catholic University?

A. Evanston-born Walter Kerr, husband of writer Jean Kerr.

Q. What was the usual price for a novel at bookstores during the Christmas season in 1911?

A. Between $1.20 and $1.40.

Q. In what year did Richard Locher, cartoonist for the Chicago *Tribune* win a Pulitzer Prize for his work?

A. 1983.

Q. In 1895, Mary McCoy won $100 for creating how many words from the phrase: "The Chicago *Daily Tribune*, Only One Cent"?

A. 14,101.

Q. The Robie House in Chicago is one of the most celebrated examples of what style of house developed by Frank Lloyd Wright in the early 1900s?

A. Prairie Style.

Q. What professor of English at Northwestern University won a Pulitzer Prize in 1964 for his work *Henry Adams: The Major Phase*?

A. Ernest Samuels.

———◆———

Q. Sarah Bernhardt set a box-office record for a two-week run in what play?

A. Rostand's *L'Aiglon*, at the Studebaker in Chicago, in October 1910.

———◆———

Q. What historian and educator, born in Camp Point and a graduate of the University of Illinois, twice was awarded the Pulitzer Prize in biography and wrote more than fifty other volumes dealing with U.S. history?

A. Allan Nevins.

———◆———

Q. What native of Illinois poet described Chicago as "Hog butcher for the world"?

A. Carl Sandburg.

———◆———

Q. What German-born member of the famed Chicago school of architecture made significant contributions to architectural engineering, acoustics, and theory and worked in partnership with Louis Sullivan?

A. Dankmar Adler.

———◆———

Q. What nationally known playboy and publisher was born in Chicago?

A. Hugh Hefner.

———◆———

Q. Ft. Sheridan native Sam Shepard won the 1979 Pulitzer Prize in drama for what play about a disintegrating family in Illinois?

A. *Buried Child*.

Q. What Chicago-born author wrote *The Cliff-Dwellers* in the late 1800s, a novel about social and financial life in Chicago?

A. Henry Blake Fuller.

--------◆--------

Q. Cartoonist Bill Mauldin, creator of the characters Willie and Joe during World War II and twice winner of the Pulitzer Prize for editorial cartooning, left the Chicago *Sun-Times* to retire in what state?

A. His native New Mexico.

--------◆--------

Q. What Illinois-born journalist, war correspondent, and radio commentator wrote *The Rise and Fall of the Third Reich*, published in 1960?

A. William Shirer.

--------◆--------

Q. What Illinois-born writer won the Pulitzer Prize in 1937 for his work *Pedlar's Progress: The Life of Bronson Alcott*?

A. Odell Shepard.

--------◆--------

Q. What Chicago author wrote *Consenting Adults, or The Duchess Will Be Furious*, a story with a lively plot set in Illinois?

A. Peter De Vries.

--------◆--------

Q. Although it moved to New York in 1918, in what year was *The Dial*, a journal of literary criticism, founded in Chicago?

A. 1880.

--------◆--------

Q. What professor of English at the University of Chicago wrote *The Common Lot*, a tale of a young Chicago architect?

A. Robert Herrick.

Q. Chicago-born proletarian novelist Albert Halper wrote what collection of semi-autobiographical sketches of Chicago?

A. *On the Shore* (1934).

———◆———

Q. What Chicago author of *The Box of God* and *Covenant with Earth* taught English at the University of Illinois and Northwestern?

A. Lew Sarett.

———◆———

Q. Who runs Bookman's Alley in Evanston, which contains books for sale and a collection of curios which are not for sale?

A. Roger Carlson, a former advertising man.

———◆———

Q. What Chicago poet and novelist wrote the collection of poems titled *The Earth-Bound*?

A. Janet Lewis.

———◆———

Q. Who wrote *The Fourth Estate*, which played at the Grand Opera House in Chicago in late December 1909, and which Percy Hammond (*Tribune*) called "Dignified . . . with a mission"?

A. Harriet Ford and Joseph Medill Patterson, then a *Tribune* executive.

———◆———

Q. Who is the present director of the Chicago Symphony Orchestra?

A. Daniel Barenboim.

———◆———

Q. Who was the first black woman to have a play, *A Raisin in the Sun*, produced on Broadway?

A. Chicago-born Lorraine Hansbury.

Q. What University of Chicago professor collaborated with Robert Maynard Hutchins, the university's president, in starting the Great Books program in 1952?

A. Mortimer Adler.

———◆———

Q. What Chicago-born novelist wrote *The Golden Watch*, a work about a boy growing up in Chicago before World War I?

A. Albert Halper.

———◆———

Q. What Chicago *Daily News* book editor became a rare book dealer?

A. The late Van Allen Bradley, author of *Gold in Your Attic*.

———◆———

Q. What Illinois-born author won a Pulitzer Prize in 1958 for his book *The Travels of Jamie McPheeters*?

A. Robert Lewis Taylor.

———◆———

Q. Morris Birkbeck, who emigrated to Illinois from England in 1817, attracted attention to the prairie region with what two works?

A. *Notes on a Journey . . . to the Territory of Illinois* and *Letters from Illinois*.

———◆———

Q. What New York-born bohemian member of a literary group that flourished in Chicago after World War I published the *Chicago Literary Times*?

A. Ben Hecht.

———◆———

Q. Published in Chicago, what is the world's largest-selling encyclopedia?

A. *World Book Encyclopedia*.

Q. What Chicago attorney wrote the bestselling *Presumed Innocent*?

A. Scott Turow.

———◆———

Q. What book published by the University of Chicago Press has aided authors, editors, and publishers nationwide since 1969?

A. *The Chicago Manual of Style*.

———◆———

Q. What prominent American composer was born in Illinois?

A. J. A. Carpenter.

———◆———

Q. What self-educated black author migrated to Chicago at age nineteen and later wrote the nationally acclaimed *Native Son*, the story of a black youth reared in Chicago's slums?

A. Richard Wright.

———◆———

Q. In what year did the Museum of Contemporary Art open?

A. 1967, and it doubled in size within a decade.

———◆———

Q. What graduate of the University of Chicago wrote *Citizens*, an analysis of the Chicago Little Steel strike and Memorial Day "massacre" of 1937?

A. Meyer Levin.

———◆———

Q. Who is the November Man?

A. The protagonist of several thrillers by Chicagoan Bill Granger.

Q. What cartoonist of the strip "Shoe" won a Pulitzer Prize for his work at the Chicago *Tribune* in 1985?

A. Jeffrey K. MacNelly.

———◆———

Q. While writing advertising copy in Chicago, who was encouraged by Carl Sandburg and Floyd Dell to publish his first book, *Windy MacPherson's Son*?

A. Sherwood Anderson.

———◆———

Q. Who compiled the *Dictionary of Quotations* published in 1968?

A. Prof. Bergen Evans of Northwestern University.

———◆———

Q. Sculptor Malvina Hoffman, a pupil of Rodin, did what series for the Field Museum of Natural History?

A. The Races of Man display.

———◆———

Q. What former professor of English at the University of Chicago edited *The Dial* after it moved to New York from Chicago in 1918?

A. Robert Morss Lovett.

———◆———

Q. One of the most famous characters in literature, Tarzan, was created by what Oak Park resident?

A. Edgar Rice Burroughs.

———◆———

Q. What novelette about a black woman's romance in Chicago was written by award-winning Gwendolyn Brooks?

A. *Maud Martha.*

Q. What novel by Upton Sinclair about the Chicago meat-packing industry prompted a federal investigation that led to the passage of pure-food legislation?

A. *The Jungle.*

Q. In what city did L. Frank Baum write *The Wonderful Wizard of Oz*?

A. Chicago, where he lived for almost twenty years.

Q. What Ft. Sheridan-born playwright wrote the screenplay for Antonioni's *Zabriski Point*?

A. Sam Shepard.

Q. What Illinois newspaper has won the Pulitzer Prize for meritorious public service three different years?

A. The Chicago *Daily-News* (1950, 1957, and 1963).

Q. What is the title of Claudia Cassidy's collection of music and drama criticism?

A. *Europe on the Aisle.*

Q. Chicago boasts what three notable dance companies in the United States as listed by the *World Almanac*?

A. Hubbard Street Dance Company, Joseph Holmes Dance Theater, and Mordine & Company.

Q. Which Chicago publication was listed among the top ten U.S. daily newspapers in 1990?

A. The Chicago *Tribune.*

SPORTS & LEISURE

C H A P T E R   F I V E

Q. How far did the winner of a women's six-day bike race pedal in 1897?

A. Over 240 miles.

Q. Mary Rose Potter, Northwestern dean of women, forbade students to dance what specific dance in 1915?

A. The waltz.

Q. What was the year of the last all-Chicago World Series?

A. 1906.

Q. What Chicago Bears running back has the most rushing yards in NFL history and was the National Football Conference leading rusher from 1976 to 1980?

A. Walter Payton.

Q. When the National Hockey League teams named "celebrity co-captains" in 1991 to observe the league's seventy-fifth year, whom did the Blackhawks pick?

A. Jim Belushi.

Q. Barbara Ann Scott, who won an Olympic figure-skating gold medal for Canada, is married to what Chicago sports and business leader?

A. Tom King.

Q. In 1899, what was the site of the bizarre billiard match when twelve-year-old Willie Hoppe beat the country's best balkline player, Al Taylor, who then gave up billiards and went to Colorado to take up mining?

A. The luxurious American Billiard Academy, Chicago.

Q. At the twelfth Little League world series in 1958, the team from what Illinois city was defeated by a team from Monterrey, Mexico?

A. Kankakee.

Q. What victory did Chicago women win in April, 1916?

A. They could wear bloomer bathing suits without stockings on the summer beaches.

Q. What major sports figure arrived too late to board the excursion boat *Eastland*, which capsized in the Chicago River in 1915 with the loss of 812 lives?

A. George Halas, later owner/coach of the Chicago Bears.

Q. What University of Chicago quarterback was on Walter Camp's All-American football team in 1910?

A. Walter Eckersall.

Q. When did the first U.S. gasoline-automobile race take place?

A. Thanksgiving Day 1895, Chicago to Evanston.

Q. What happened when Notre Dame introduced the University of Chicago to the Princeton place-kick in 1917?

A. The Irish beat the Maroons for the first time, in Chicago.

———◆———

Q. What feat did Edward Payson Weston, the world's champion walker, accomplish in 1909 at the age of seventy?

A. Walked from New York to San Francisco in 104 days, 7 hours.

———◆———

Q. What Chicagoan won the National Open Golf Tournament in Minneapolis in June 1916?

A. Charles ("Chick") Evans, Jr.

———◆———

Q. What Chicago prizefighter was the U.S. bantamweight champion in 1897?

A. Jimmy Barry.

———◆———

Q. The Chicago Cubs won the World Series what two years?

A. 1907 and 1908.

———◆———

Q. Joliet-born basketball great George Mikan signed with what team for $60,000 for five years in 1947?

A. The National League Chicago American Gears.

———◆———

Q. Who won the one-, five-, and eight-mile auto race at the Libertyville track August 9, 1913?

A. Eddie Rickenbacker, the future World War I aviation ace.

Q. Who made the first aerial drop over Lake Michigan July 1, 1913?

A. Jack Vilas and a passenger in a flying-boat.

———◆———

Q. What stadium is home to the Chicago Bears football team?

A. Soldier Field.

———◆———

Q. In what year did horse-racing resume at Hawthorne after a twelve-year ban?

A. 1916.

———◆———

Q. Balloon Classic Illinois takes place on the second week-end following Memorial Day at what city?

A. Danville.

———◆———

Q. Chicago Bears kicker Kevin Butler completed at least one field goal in how many consecutive games?

A. Twenty-three, during the 1988-89 season.

———◆———

Q. In September 1897, when the Chicago Golf Club at Wheaton hosted the largest men's golf tourney ever staged outside of the East, who won the U.S. Amateur match play event?

A. H. J. Whigham of Onwentsia beat W. R. Betts of Shinne-cock Hills.

———◆———

Q. How many cycling enthusiasts attended the bicycle show at Tattersall's in Chicago in January 1895?

A. The week-long spectacle drew 90,000.

Q. Why did Dr. Otto Schneider, president in 1908 of the Chicago Board of Education, call high school sports "a national disease"?

A. Because "sport doesn't educate."

Q. How many fans watched the White Sox lose to St. Louis, 2-0, in the first game played in the new Comiskey Park July 1, 1910?

A. 28,000.

Q. How did Chick Evans celebrate his return from a European tour in 1911?

A. He smashed the amateur scoring record at Edgewater with a seventy-one, seven strokes below the old mark.

Q. How did the Cubs get within half a game of the league-leading Giants on September 21, 1908?

A. Mordecai Brown won both ends of a double-header.

Q. When did boxing become legal in Chicago?

A. October 23, 1897.

Q. What city alderman tried to have football banned in Chicago in 1897?

A. Nathan Plotke (the ordinance was defeated 57 to 5).

Q. What was Ralph De Palma's average speed when he won the 301-mile Elgin National in his Mercedes in 1914?

A. 73.5 miles per hour.

Q. While celebrating its railroad heritage in late spring, what town sponsors a spike-driving contest?

A. Galesburg, during Galesburg Railroad Days.

Q. How much stock in the Cubs did William Wrigley buy in December 1916?

A. $15,000 worth, bringing the total value of his stock to $165,000.

Q. Who won the six-day bicycle race at Tattersall's in Chicago in February 1897?

A. Fred Schinneer, who pedaled 1,788 miles for $1,000.

Q. One of the most valuable motorcycles in the country, a 1930s Harley Davidson with only 400 original miles, is on display at what museum near Mount Vernon?

A. Dale's Classic Car and Motorcycle Museum.

Q. What team defeated the Cubs in the 1910 World Series?

A. The Athletics, in five games.

Q. Who beat a baseball team from Waseda, Japan, in 1911 in Chicago?

A. The University of Chicago, 6 to 4.

Q. What was the membership limit of the Indian Hill Golf Club which opened in Winnetka on July 11, 1914?

A. Two hundred.

Q. When did the Chicago Bulls win the National Basketball Association title for the first time in the club's history?

A. 1991.

───────◆───────

Q. How many times have the Chicago Cubs lost the World Series?

A. Eight (1906, 1910, 1918, 1929, 1932, 1935, 1938, 1945).

───────◆───────

Q. What honor did Michael Jordan of the Chicago Bulls win in 1985?

A. National Basketball Association Rookie of the Year.

───────◆───────

Q. After Exmoor Country Club in Highland Park opened on June 1, 1897, who won the first tournament?

A. G. A. McKinlock, who shot 109 for 18 holes.

───────◆───────

Q. Why did James Hart, president of the Cubs, sign a larceny complaint against a fan in 1905?

A. The man caught a foul ball and kept it.

───────◆───────

Q. How many persons attended the 1910 Chicago auto show?

A. 320,000, who spent more than $2 million.

───────◆───────

Q. When was the new Skokie Country Club main building opened?

A. May 21, 1898.

Q. What member of the Chicago Cubs was the first Canadian-born player elected to the Hall of Fame?

A. Ferguson Jenkins.

Q. What event did the exclusive Riding Club of Onwentsia stage September 6, 1900?

A. Its version of an English fox hunt.

Q. What pitcher beat St. Louis, 3-2 and 2-0, on July 1, 1905?

A. Frank Owen, who won twenty-one games for the White Sox that year.

Q. From what source did the Harper Memorial Library of the University of Chicago obtain a gift of $2,500 in 1909?

A. The school's athletic department, which had cleared $5,000 on football in 1908.

Q. What was the career record of Mordecai Brown, the Cubs great who made the National Baseball Hall of Fame in 1949?

A. Won, 229; lost, 131; ERA, 2.06.

Q. When the University of Chicago met Purdue in the 1908 football season opener, who won?

A. The Chicago Maroons beat the Purdue Boilermakers, 39-0.

Q. In 1984, what was the score when Illinois played UCLA in the Rose Bowl?

A. UCLA, 45; Illinois, 9.

Q. Who was the Masters Bowling Tournament champion in 1986?

A. Mark Fahy of Chicago.

Q. Who became unofficial football champions of the West by beating Wisconsin, 18-12, on November 21, 1908?

A. The University of Chicago.

Q. Chicago golfer Chick Evans made it three in a row by winning what event in June 1909?

A. The Western Intercollegiate Golf Tournament.

Q. What plans did Charles A. Comiskey announce September 4, 1909?

A. The building of a new fireproof ballpark seating 30,000.

Q. Cuban-born Carola Mandel, wife of Chicagoan Leon Mandel, gained some notoriety for what reason?

A. She was a world-class rifle shot.

Q. What salary did Three Finger Brown demand of the Cubs' management in November 1909, after he had won twenty-six games?

A. $6,000 a year.

Q. What Chicago-born high school dropout was the first American to win the official world chess championship?

A. Bobby Fischer, who won the title in 1972 by defeating defending champion Boris Spassky of the Soviet Union in the most publicized chess match in history.

Q. Upon retirement, Waukegan native Otto Graham, the Cleveland Browns great quarterback, accepted what sports position?

A. Coach of the U.S. Coast Guard Academy football team.

◆

Q. What White Sox pitcher in the 1950s, when asked if he would throw at his mother if she were at bat, answered, "Only if she was crowding the plate"?

A. Early Wynn.

◆

Q. What did P. K. Wrigley do when the Cubs were out of first place for sixteen straight years?

A. He hired several managers, letting each manage part of the 1962 season, and the team lost 103 games, a new low.

◆

Q. What double feat did Lou Boudreau, a native of Harvey, accomplish in 1948?

A. He was the American League's Most Valuable Player, and he also managed Cleveland to a World Series victory.

◆

Q. Who was the Big Ten Conference football champion in 1983?

A. The University of Illinois.

◆

Q. How did Robert A. Gardner of Hinsdale, the national amateur golf champion, fare in the Glen View Invitational Tournament in August 1910?

A. He beat fifty-year-old Walter J. Travis, of Garden City, New York, one-up in 37 holes.

◆

Q. Who won the Illinois Athletic Club marathon, Ravinia to the club, September 19, 1908, twenty-five miles in 2:57:30?

A. Albert A. Corey, first in the field of seventy-nine.

Q. What Hall of Fame pitcher, who won forty-six games and lost twelve for Chicago in 1876, presented his collection of baseball memorabilia to the University of Chicago in 1908?

A. Albert Goodwill Spalding.

Q. How did the Chicago Whales of the Federal League fare in the 1910 season opener?

A. They beat the St. Louis Feds, 3-1.

Q. What famous double-play combination, which has become part of baseball lore, involved three Chicago Cubs players?

A. (Joe) Tinker to (Johnny) Evers to (Frank) Chance.

Q. What speed did Charles Merz average, to win the 203-mile Elgin road race in 1912?

A. A new record of 66 miles per hour.

Q. How many times have the Chicago White Sox lost the World Series?

A. Two (1919 and 1959).

Q. What football great celebrated his one hundredth birthday August 16, 1962?

A. Amos Alonzo Stagg, who had quit coaching only three years before.

Q. After Jimmy Barry of Chicago won the bantamweight championship bout by a knockout over Walter Croot in December 1897, what happened to Barry?

A. He was charged with manslaughter, temporarily, because Croot died the day after the prizefight.

Q. The University of Chicago won the intercollegiate basketball title in 1908 by beating what team?

A. The University of Pennsylvania, 16-15.

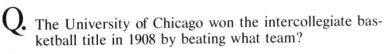

Q. What White Sox outfielder said "They can hit me, but they can't keep me away from the plate," after getting a hairline fracture from a pitched ball?

A. Minnie Minoso.

Q. When wrestling champion Farmer Gotch and Chief War Eagle met in October 1907 at Brooke's Casino, who won?

A. The farmer beat the eagle.

Q. How long did it take Montague Roberts in a Thomas Flyer to drive from New York to Chicago in February 1907?

A. Thirteen days, because of a huge snowstorm in Indiana.

Q. How many cycling enthusiasts attended the bicycle show at Tattersall's in Chicago January 1895?

A. The week-long spectacle drew 90,000.

Q. The Chicago White Sox won the World Series what two years?

A. 1906 and 1917.

Q. What was the 1986 Super Bowl score?

A. Chicago Bears, 46; New England Patriots, 10.

Q. What is the nickname of the Western Illinois University football team?

A. Leathernecks.

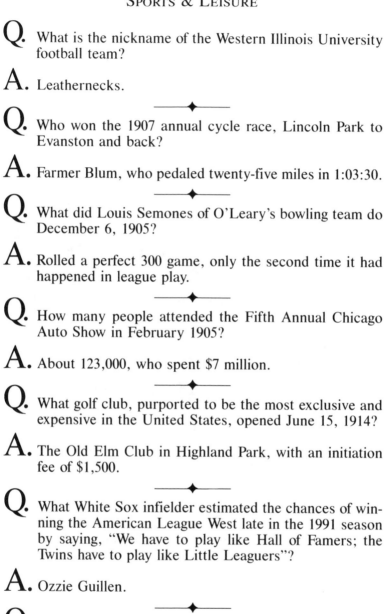

Q. Who won the 1907 annual cycle race, Lincoln Park to Evanston and back?

A. Farmer Blum, who pedaled twenty-five miles in 1:03:30.

Q. What did Louis Semones of O'Leary's bowling team do December 6, 1905?

A. Rolled a perfect 300 game, only the second time it had happened in league play.

Q. How many people attended the Fifth Annual Chicago Auto Show in February 1905?

A. About 123,000, who spent $7 million.

Q. What golf club, purported to be the most exclusive and expensive in the United States, opened June 15, 1914?

A. The Old Elm Club in Highland Park, with an initiation fee of $1,500.

Q. What White Sox infielder estimated the chances of winning the American League West late in the 1991 season by saying, "We have to play like Hall of Famers; the Twins have to play like Little Leaguers"?

A. Ozzie Guillen.

Q. What was the origin of White Sox pitcher Mordecai Brown's nickname "Three Finger"?

A. He lacked the index finger on his right hand.

Q. How did University of Chicago quarterback Pete Russell beat Purdue single-footed on October 25, 1913?

A. He drop-kicked two field goals.

Q. What ordinance did the city council of Chicago vote down on March 23, 1914?

A. One that banned free beer at the theater, sporting events, and on streetcars.

Q. What did Charles L. Buel accomplish by walking from Trevor, Wisconsin, to the stockyards, covering the sixty miles in thirteen and one-half hours on May 20, 1899?

A. He beat a stock train by four hours, winning a $500 bet.

Q. How many fans witnessed the Chicago Cubs defeat St. Louis, on March 29, 1899?

A. 27,489, the largest crowd to date to watch a baseball game in Chicago.

Q. How many points did Michael Jordan of the Chicago Bulls score in 1991?

A. 2,580.

Q. Where did Decatur native Chuck Dressen play baseball before making the big leagues?

A. Moline, as an infielder in 1919.

Q. What was the name of the St. Charles women's softball team that won the 1977 major slow pitch championship?

A. Fox Valley Lassies.

Q. To what conference does the Eastern Illinois University football team belong?

A. Gateway.

———◆———

Q. On February 18, 1990, Martina Navratilova won what tennis tournament held in Chicago?

A. Virginia Slims.

———◆———

Q. What Chicagoan was the smallest player ever to bat in a major league game?

A. Eddie Gaedel, standing three feet, seven inches tall, and weighing sixty-five pounds, who was put in as a pinch-hitter for the St. Louis Browns in 1951.

———◆———

Q. The University of Chicago played in the Big Ten conference since it began in 1895 until 1940 when Chicago withdrew, having won how many championships during that time?

A. Six.

———◆———

Q. Who coached the Chicago Blackhawks in 1961?

A. Rudy Pilous.

———◆———

Q. In 1982, what was the score when Illinois played Alabama in the Liberty Bowl?

A. Alabama, 21; Illinois, 15.

———◆———

Q. Who won the first Heisman Trophy in 1935?

A. Jay Berwanger, University of Chicago halfback.

—153—

Q. What two Northwestern coaches won College Football Coach of the Year awards?

A. Lynn Waldorf in 1935 and Alex Agase in 1970.

———◆———

Q. What outstanding, and highly controversial, baseball manager never made the Hall of Fame?

A. The late Leo Durocher, who was with four teams during his major league playing career, including six years with the Chicago Cubs (1966-72).

———◆———

Q. In 1920, Chuck Dressen was quarterback for what team that later was called the Chicago Bears?

A. The Decatur Staleys.

———◆———

Q. What suggestion in Kup's column in November 1991, was picked up immediately by the Atlanta Braves and Chicago Blackhawks?

A. That professional teams with Indian names should offer scholarships to native Americans.

———◆———

Q. Competing for the eleventh time, what Chicago attorney was the oldest contestant in the 1991 Chicago Marathon?

A. Art McLendon, age seventy-five, who finished in seven hours.

———◆———

Q. What record does Sid Luckman of the Chicago Bears share with four other NFL quarterbacks?

A. Passing for seven touchdowns in a single game.

———◆———

Q. What Chicago Cardinals football player caught five touchdown passes in one game?

A. Bob Shaw, in the Chicago-Baltimore game in 1950.

Q. What baseball song, which appeared in 1817, was dedicated to the Atlantic Club of Chicago?

A. "Home Run Galop".

Q. When was the Rockford baseball team organized?

A. In 1865, with sixteen-year-old A. G. Spalding pitching.

Q. Hale Irwin won the U.S. Open golf tournament on June 17, 1990, at what Illinois course?

A. Medinah.

Q. Who was the U.S. Ladies Curling champion in 1982?

A. Ruth Schwenker of Illinois.

Q. The Blue Demons is the nickname of what Illinois university basketball team?

A. DePaul.

Q. Although the Washington Nationals baseball team defeated the famous Chicago Excelsiors, 49-4, July 26, 1867, what team had beaten them the previous day?

A. Rockford, 29-23.

Q. Chicagoan Chick Evans won what golf title for the third straight time at Grand Rapids, August 1, 1914?

A. The Western Amateur championship playing against James Standish, Jr., of Detroit.

Q. With whom did future baseball great Walter Johnson sign a two-year contract at an estimated annual salary of $20,000, in December 1914?

A. The Chifeds of the Chicago Federal League, but two weeks later he broke his agreement and went with the Washington Senators.

Q. What member of the Baseball Hall of Fame, a White Sox shortstop for twenty years, was nicknamed Old Aches and Pains?

A. Luke Appling.

Q. Before almost every game, the perennial cry of what Cubs infielder was "It's a great day! Let's play two!"?

A. Ernie Banks.

Q. Who has been the Cubs' equipment manager since 1943?

A. Yosh Kawano.

Q. What was the score of the most one-sided football game in National League History?

A. The Chicago Bears, 73; Washington Redskins, 0, on December 8, 1940.

Q. What was the score in the first game played in the new Comiskey Park April 18, 1991?

A. Detroit Tigers, 16; Chicago White Sox, 1.

Q. A photograph of what member of the 1919 "Black Sox" hangs on the wall of Comiskey Park?

A. "Shoeless" Joe Jackson.

Q. What member of the Hall of Fame was the Chicago Bears longest-playing quarterback?

A. Sid Luckman, 1939-1950.

———◆———

Q. When did the Chicago *Tribune* become owners of the Chicago Cubs?

A. In June 1981.

———◆———

Q. What Chicago White Sox player was the only player ever chosen for All-Star teams in baseball and football?

A. Bo Jackson, although injury kept him from the NFL All-Star football team.

———◆———

Q. What Chicago Cubs player set the all-time record for runs-batted-in during a single season?

A. Hack Wilson, 190 RBI in 155 games, in 1930.

———◆———

Q. What Chicago Cardinals player holds the single-player record for scoring in a game?

A. Ernie Nevers, with forty points in the Cardinals-Bears game, November 28, 1929.

———◆———

Q. How many games did Robert (Bobby) Thigpen save for the Chicago White Sox in 1990?

A. A record fifty-seven.

———◆———

Q. How many times have the Chicago Blackhawks won the Stanley Cup?

A. Three (1934, 1938, 1961).

Q. What is the longest game ever played in time-consumed?

A. Chicago White Sox vs. Milwaukee Brewers, with elapsed time of eight hours, six minutes (the May 9, 1984, tied game was halted because of the 1:00 A.M. curfew and when resumed the following day the White Sox won, 7-6).

———◆———

Q. What is the World Series attendance record for all games in a series?

A. 420,784 for the 1950 series, Dodgers vs. White Sox.

———◆———

Q. Illinois native Charles Mellor won the Boston Marathon with a time of 2:33:08 in what year?

A. 1925.

———◆———

Q. What two Chicago Blackhawks took possession of the Hart Memorial Trophy for most valuable player in hockey for four consecutive years?

A. Bobby Hull (1965-66) and Stan Mikita (1967-68).

———◆———

Q. What former running back and tackle for the Chicago Bears died in International Falls, Minnesota in January 1990?

A. Bronko Nagurski, three-time All-Pro who helped lead the Bears to three NFL titles (1932, 1933, 1943).

———◆———

Q. What two fighters were in the World Heavyweight Championship held in Chicago September 22, 1927?

A. Gene Tunney (victor) and Jack Dempsey.

———◆———

Q. In what year did the Archer Daniels Midland men's softball team from Decatur win the major fast pitch national championship?

A. 1981.

Q. What honor did Gale Sayers, Chicago Bears running back, win in 1965?

A. Rookie of the Year.

———◆———

Q. What Chicago Bears player was the outstanding linebacker in the NFL in 1969 and 1970?

A. Dick Butkus.

———◆———

Q. In 1942, what Northwestern football player set a Big Ten passing record with 89 completions in 182 tries?

A. Otto Graham.

———◆———

Q. In what year did Chicago Bulls Dick Motta win the Red Auerbach Trophy for outstanding coach of the year?

A. 1971.

———◆———

Q. What Chicago television personality led the NFL in pass-catching in 1964?

A. Johnny Morris (93 for 1,200 yards and 10 touchdowns).

———◆———

Q. What hockey player has had his number retired by both the Chicago Blackhawks and the Winnipeg Jets?

A. Bobby Hull, #9.

———◆———

Q. In what two years did Gale Sayers of the Chicago Bears hold the NFL rushing title?

A. 1966 and 1969.

Q. Bob Elson, an announcer for the White Sox games over forty-five years ago, had what off-season job?

A. Interviewing celebrity guests at the Pump Room.

——◆——

Q. In what year did Joe Louis win the World Heavyweight Championship against defender James J. Braddock in Chicago?

A. 1937.

——◆——

Q. In what game did University of Illinois halfback Harold E. ("Red") Grange earn his name of Galloping Ghost?

A. Against Michigan, October 18, 1924, when he raced for four touchdowns in twelve minutes in the opening quarter of the game, then in the last quarter ran for a fifth and passed for his sixth.

——◆——

Q. What boxer beat Carmen Basilio in the Chicago Stadium on March 15, 1958, to regain his middleweight title for the fourth time?

A. Sugar Ray Robinson.

——◆——

Q. What Hall of Fame shortstop never played in a World Series during sixteen seasons at shortstop and first base with the Chicago Cubs?

A. Ernie Banks, who hit 474 home runs during that stretch.

——◆——

Q. What mark did Bob Parsons of the Chicago Bears set in 1981?

A. Most punts in a single season: 114.

——◆——

Q. What late president of Marine Bank in Champaign-Urbana had been an NFL referee since 1971, with twelve postseason playoff games including Super Bowl XXIV?

A. Dick Jorgensen.

Q. What All-Star game was held in Chicago Stadium on January 19, 1991?

A. The National Hockey League.

———◆———

Q. What is the NFL record for consecutive victories?

A. Eighteen, held by the Chicago Bears and two other teams.

———◆———

Q. The Atlanta Hawks were once called the Tri-Cities Blackhawks and held franchises in what three cities?

A. Moline and Rock Island, Illinois, and Davenport, Iowa (1946–1951).

———◆———

Q. What NFL coach has won the most games to date?

A. George Halas of the Bears with a record of 325-151-31 and seven NFL championships.

———◆———

Q. When Pres. A. W. Harris announced in 1907 that Northwestern had the largest student body of any university in the country, what coincidence did he point out?

A. That the enrollment jump came with the abolishment of intercollegiate football at NU.

———◆———

Q. What major football upset did the Northwestern Wildcats bring off during 1991?

A. They beat the Illini 20-17, for their first Big Ten victory of the season.

———◆———

Q. What scoring record did the University of Chicago baseball team bring back in December 1915 from a tour of China, Japan, and the Philippines?

A. Thirty-three games won and seven lost.

Q. What yacht finished first in the twelve-yacht field in July 1909, to win the annual Chicago-Mackinaw race for the second straight year?

A. The *Valmore*, owned by William ("Big Bill") Thompson.

Q. Rev. E. B. Stewart, a Presbyterian minister, made what complaint in 1905 about South Park board officials?

A. Permitting sports activities on the Sabbath.

Q. The Chicago Bears hold the record for how many fumbles made by a professional team in one season?

A. Fifty-six, in 1938.

Q. In October 1909, when Glenn Curtiss circled the Hawthorne racetrack in an airplane, how high did he fly?

A. Sixty to one hundred feet.

Q. What year did the Chicago White Sox defeat the Chicago Cubs, four games to two, in the World Series?

A. 1906.

Q. Why was a permit for a public euchre party in Wilmette, with hand-painted china as prizes, denied in September 1915?

A. It might be considered gambling.

Q. What diversions did Mayor Harrison ban in 1897 in an attempt to clean up the city?

A. Prizefighting and gambling.

Q. What Chicago team has retired the most numbers for any team in its league?

A. Chicago Bears, 10.

———◆———

Q. What happened to a Chicago balloonist entertaining a crowd on July 26, 1911, over Plainfield?

A. He fell seven hundred feet while performing on the trapeze.

———◆———

Q. In 1989, what baseball broadcaster won the Ford Frick Award for meritorious contributions to broadcasting?

A. Harry Caray, sportscaster for the Chicago Cubs.

———◆———

Q. What ban did the Onwentsia golf club relax on July 22, 1917, that all other golf clubs already had done?

A. Permitted Sunday play.

———◆———

Q. What record does Dorothy Gaters of Maywood have as coach of Chicago's Marshall High School girls' basketball team?

A. Her team won city championships from 1978 through 1990 and was beaten in 1991 in overtime.

———◆———

Q. What three former Negro League baseball stars signed autographs at the Twelfth Sports Collectors Convention in Chicago in November 1991?

A. Jimmie Crutchfield, Ted ("Double Duty") Radcliff, and Lester Lockett.

———◆———

Q. What is the nickname of the Eastern Illinois University football team?

A. Panthers.

Q. What St. Charles resident won the Miss America body-building title in Atlantic City in October 1991 and the next week in London was fourth in the Miss Universe competition?

A. Terri LoCicero of St. Charles.

———————◆———————

Q. Where have Northwestern University's players competed overseas?

A. Switzerland, Italy, Greece, Japan, and England.

———————◆———————

Q. What football legend coached the University of Chicago football team for forty-one years, including five undefeated seasons and introduced the huddle, man-in-motion, and the end-around play?

A. Amos Alonzo Stagg.

———————◆———————

Q. When did the new Woman's Athletic Club open at 606 South Michigan Avenue in Chicago?

A. January 16, 1909.

———————◆———————

Q. The Chicago Bulls have retired one number in their history for what player?

A. Jerry Sloan, #4.

———————◆———————

Q. What was the *Sun-Times* sports-page headline December 23, 1991, after the Bears were routed by the San Francisco Forty-Niners, and were to lose the division title as well as a better spot in the race to the Super Bowl?

A. "BYE-BYE, BYE."

———————◆———————

Q. Devotees of what sport may practice indoors south of the Loop, under a huge tent atop an old railway terminal?

A. Golf, at a driving range.

Q. When was the Chicago Bulls first season of play?

A. 1966-67.

━━━━━◆━━━━━

Q. Who coached the Tri-Cities Blackhawks from 1949-50?

A. Red Auerbach.

━━━━━◆━━━━━

Q. Who wrote *The Bingo Long Traveling All-Stars and Motor Kings*, a tale about black baseball teams before Jackie Robinson lowered the color barrier?

A. Bill Brashler, a Chicago author who recently has been collaborating on a series of baseball mysteries.

━━━━━◆━━━━━

Q. What curious feat did Andre Dawson accomplish during the 1991 baseball season?

A. He hit two grand slams in the same series—and the Cubs lost both games.

━━━━━◆━━━━━

Q. On August 20, 1915, the Chicago White Sox traded three players to the Cleveland Indians for what *one* of their players?

A. "Shoeless" Joe Jackson.

━━━━━◆━━━━━

Q. When did the Washington Bullets represent Chicago?

A. 1961-63, the first two years of the Bullets' franchise.

━━━━━◆━━━━━

Q. In 1953, what two boxers were in the World Heavyweight Championship in Chicago?

A. Rocky Marciano beat Jersey Joe Walcott by a knockout.

Q. What golfers participate in the Eskimo Open, which has been held in Chicago each winter for over thirty years?

A. A group of weatherproof golfers who turn out on the designated Sunday regardless of meteorological conditions.

————◆————

Q. The ballplayer-evangelist Billy Sunday, once regarded as the fastest man in baseball, stole how many bases in 1890?

A. A record eighty-three, which Ty Cobb equaled in 1911 and smashed in 1915.

————◆————

Q. What native of Peoria has done play-by-play of 5,300 major league ball games, eight of them no-hit, no-run contests?

A. Jack Brickhouse, long-time sportscaster for WGN-TV.

————◆————

Q. How many times did Chicago Blackhawks center Stan Mikita lead the National Hockey League in scoring?

A. Four.

————◆————

Q. When Jim Essian, interim Cubs manager in 1991, was let go with his contract still running through the 1992 baseball season, what job did he take?

A. Scout for the Cubs in the Detroit area, beginning in January 1992.

————◆————

Q. Who was the son of Charles Evans, author of most of the "American Bibliography," and former head of the Chicago Historical Society?

A. Charles ("Chick") Evans, Jr., noted golfer.

————◆————

Q. What former outfielder for the Chicago National League used his baseball background, slangy language, and flamboyant style to become a popular evangelist, credited with converting over a million people in his gospel campaigns?

A. William Ashley ("Billy") Sunday.

Q. What veteran player did the Cubs release in 1916?

A. Mordecai ("Three Finger") Brown.

———◆———

Q. What four Blackhawks players have had their numbers retired?

A. Glenn Hull, #1; Bobby Hull, #9; Stan Mikita, #21; Tony Esposito, #35.

———◆———

Q. In what two years did the Chicago Cardinals win their only NFL championships?

A. 1925 and 1947.

———◆———

Q. To what two clubs in Illinois was the baseball song "Catch It On the Fly" dedicated?

A. The Excelsior Club of Chicago and the Forest City Club of Rockford.

———◆———

Q. What was the lifetime batting average of Luke Appling of the Chicago White Sox?

A. .310 (he hit over .300 for nine consecutive years).

———◆———

Q. What is the attendance record for a game in the World Series?

A. 92,706, for the fifth game of the 1950 series, Dodgers vs. White Sox.

———◆———

Q. What was the name of the men's softball team from Aurora that won the Major Fast Pitch championship in 1959?

A. Sealmasters.

Q. What was the latest dance craze among North Side Chicago couples in 1912?

A. The tango.

◆

Q. When Stan Mikita of the Blackhawks retired from hockey, what sports position did he assume?

A. Director of golf at Kemper Lakes near Long Grove.

◆

Q. Chicago Bears quarterback Sid Luckman led his team to how many National Football League championships?

A. Four (1940, 1941, 1943, and 1946).

◆

Q. What was the name of the Chicago team that participated in the brief existence of the World Hockey Association (1973-79)?

A. Cougars.

◆

Q. At what age did Chicago native Bobby Fischer become the youngest international chess grandmaster in chess history?

A. Fifteen.

◆

Q. According to the Baseball Writer's Association, who was the National League's Most Valuable Player in 1984?

A. Ryne Sandberg, Chicago Cubs.

◆

Q. What Chicago player was the scoring champion in pro basketball in 1948?

A. Max Zaslofsky, 1007 points in 48 games.

Q. As of 1991, who had the highest career scoring average among players with at least 10,000 points?

A. Michael Jordan, the leading scorer in the league for five years (1987-1991), whose 16,596 points average out to 37.6 per game.

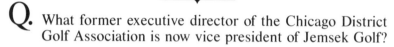

Q. What former executive director of the Chicago District Golf Association is now vice president of Jemsek Golf?

A. Carol McCue.

Q. In what year was the Chicago Bud Light Triathalon Series started?

A. 1983.

Q. What was the name of the Women's Professional Basketball League team from Chicago?

A. The Hustle.

Q. Who won the Western Open golf tournament held in Oak Brook, Illinois, on June 10, 1990?

A. Wayne Levi.

Q. Joey Sindelar won what pro golf tournament held in Coal Valley on September 9, 1990?

A. Hardee's Classic.

Q. Bonnie Blair, 1988 Winter Olympics 500-meter speed skating champion, was from what Illinois town?

A. Champaign.

Q. What was the name of the Chicago team entered in the United States Football League (USFL)?

A. The Blitz.

———◆———

Q. In what year did the Chicago Sting rout the New York Cosmos in overtime for the National American Soccer League championship?

A. 1981.

———◆———

Q. In what year was the Chicago America's Marathon started?

A. 1970.

———◆———

Q. How many fans watched the White Sox depart for their 1916 training camp in Mineral Wells, Texas?

A. About 3,000.

———◆———

Q. Where did Jane Albright, Northern Illinois University women's basketball coach, rank in the *Philadelphia Inquirer* coaches' poll for the 1989-90 season?

A. Seventeenth.

———◆———

Q. Who was the National Basketball Association's most valuable player in 1991?

A. Michael Jordan of the Chicago Bulls.

———◆———

Q. In what year did Illinois native Mike Ryan win the Boston Marathon with a time of 2:21:18?

A. 1912.

SCIENCE & NATURE

C H A P T E R S I X

Q. What is the Illinois state flower?

A. The native violet.

---◆---

Q. What is the altitude of Chicago?

A. From 579 to 673 feet above sea level.

---◆---

Q. Exactly where did the Manhattan Project's first controlled nuclear chain reaction take place in 1942?

A. In a squash-court laboratory under the football field at the University of Chicago.

---◆---

Q. Chicagoan Leonard Dubkin wrote what book describing bird, animal, or insect life unnoticed by most city-dwellers?

A. *My Secret Places.*

---◆---

Q. How long did a rainstorm in December 1895 last in Chicago?

A. Three days, leaving water twelve feet deep in some places.

Q. Of the thirteen medical schools in Chicago, a Carnegie Foundation report in 1910 found only what one to be "superior"?

A. Rush.

———◆———

Q. To what extremes did the temperature reach in Chicago on November 11, 1911?

A. 74.3 degrees in mid-afternoon and 26 degrees at 2:00 A.M. the next morning after a raging thunderstorm.

———◆———

Q. A French tannery-owner on the Ohio River near what is now Grand Chain bought how many buffalo hides in 1700?

A. 31,000.

———◆———

Q. For what purpose did paint manufacturer Jules Knapp and his wife, Gwen, give $10 million to the University of Chicago in 1991?

A. To establish the Gwen Knapp Center for Lupus and Immunology Research.

———◆———

Q. The American bald eagle, red-tailed hawk, and great blue heron are likely to be seen at what state recreation area opened in 1975 near Benton?

A. Wayne Fitzgerell.

———◆———

Q. When was the last buffalo killed in Illinois?

A. Reputedly in 1808.

———◆———

Q. Other than a city in Illinois, what is galena?

A. The chief ore of lead (the city was once the center of trade for the upper Mississippi lead mine region).

Q. In 1907, what was the annual mortality rate from tuberculosis in Chicago?

A. 3,500.

———◆———

Q. What is the state tree?

A. The white oak.

———◆———

Q. What was the wind speed during the Great Fire as established by an anemometer at U.S. Weather Signal Office on LaSalle Street?

A. 60 m.p.h.

———◆———

Q. Why is the state reducing the numbers of chinook salmon introduced into Lake Michigan annually?

A. Because they eat so many alewives other game fish are finding it hard to subsist.

———◆———

Q. For what research did the late Prof. George Stigler, University of Chicago economist, win the Nobel Prize in 1982?

A. A study of markets and governmental regulations.

———◆———

Q. What was the temperature in Chicago on July 5, 1911, when forty-four people died of heat prostration?

A. 101.5 degrees.

———◆———

Q. What arboretum near Lisle covers 700 acres and has 5,000 kinds of trees and plants?

A. Morton Arboretum.

Q. Northern Illinois averages how many inches of precipitation per year?

A. Thirty-four.

Q. In what year did the first zinc smelter in Illinois start operating?

A. 1860, at LaSalle.

Q. A 1912 study showed what city of the ten largest internationally to be the healthiest?

A. Chicago, with London second.

Q. Where was the first truly successful steel plow perfected?

A. Grand Detour, in 1837, when blacksmith John Deere made a self-cleaning one.

Q. What did Dr. Leslie E. Keeley, a graduate of Rush Medical School, found in Dwight in 1890?

A. The Keeley Institute for the treatment of alcoholism.

Q. Situated on the great Mississippi flyway, Illinois hosts about how many ducks to rest and feed during the annual spring and fall migrations?

A. Two million.

Q. What LaSalle County sheriff patented the West's most popular type of barbed wire in 1892?

A. Joseph F. Glidden.

Q. What improvement in delivery service did the Charles A. Stevens Company of Chicago use in 1897?

A. The first electric wagons in the nation.

———◆———

Q. Why were Chicago schoolchildren told to bring drinking water in canteens in September 1900?

A. There was a typhoid epidemic.

———◆———

Q. What Italian-born physicist, working at the University of Chicago in 1942, headed the team that made possible the development of the atomic bomb?

A. Enrico Fermi.

———◆———

Q. What archaeological site near Lewiston displays native American artifacts *in situ*?

A. Dickson Mounds, containing a museum in a 160-acre parklike setting.

———◆———

Q. Two youngsters were admitted to Cook County Hospital in July 1916 with what disease, previously unknown in Chicago?

A. Infantile paralysis (polio).

———◆———

Q. Who succeeded Dr. Lester Fisher as head of the Lincoln Park Zoo April 1, 1992?

A. David Hales, former director of Michigan's Department of Natural Resources.

———◆———

Q. What is the state bird?

A. The cardinal.

Q. How many eggs were marketed in the state in 1990?

A. 793 million.

———◆———

Q. What are Chicago's record high and low temperatures?

A. 105 degrees on July 21, 1934, and -27 degrees on January 21, 1985.

———◆———

Q. What endangered species of bird was added to the collection at the Chicago Field Museum of Natural History in the fall of 1919?

A. A Cooper's hawk (it died when it hit a skyscraper window).

———◆———

Q. When did the first electric train arrive in downtown Chicago on the Lake Street el?

A. June 14, 1896.

———◆———

Q. The Chicago health commissioner issued what rule regarding milk in July 1916?

A. Only pasteurized milk could be sold.

———◆———

Q. To solve its serious mosquito problem, the town of Griggsville employed what natural method of insect control?

A. Situated on the migration route of purple martins, it erected 504 nesting units on a forty-foot tower to lure thousands of the insect-eating birds to summer there.

———◆———

Q. What improvement was made on Chicago's Michigan Avenue between 14th and 39th streets on September 1, 1897?

A. Electric lights replaced gas jets.

Q. Why were persons at Zion College in Chicago quarantined in March 1902?

A. One case of smallpox had been discovered and, in accordance with their beliefs, they refused vaccination.

Q. Where does Illinois rank in the nation in export of agricultural products?

A. First.

Q. What is Chicago's most popular civic attraction?

A. The Museum of Science and Industry, which draws more than four million visitors annually.

Q. What now defunct watch manufacturer used screws so minuscule that twenty thousand of them would fit into a thimble?

A. The Elgin National Watch Company.

Q. What were the Birch, Bradley, Hamlin-Holmes, Marshall, and Shaw?

A. Automobiles manufactured in Chicago in the early 1920s.

Q. What special meteorological skill does Mathon Kyritsis, Waukegan restaurant owner, possess?

A. Prediction of upcoming winter weather by observing the behavior of the lake perch.

Q. What principal founder of one of the world's largest meat-packing firms donated money in 1892 to found an institute of technology, a precursor of the Illinois Institute of Technology?

A. Philip Danforth Armour.

Q. The American Motor League, the world's first motor club, was formed in Chicago in what year?

A. 1895.

———◆———

Q. How did Chicago health instructors describe the average Chicago businessman in 1912?

A. As possessing flat feet, round shoulders, and a fat middle.

———◆———

Q. How much lead did Galena export in 1850?

A. 672,620 pigs, valued at $2,225,000.

———◆———

Q. What pioneer social scientist taught at the University of Chicago for thirty-eight years, helping establish its School of Social Service Administration in 1920?

A. Sophonsiba Breckenridge.

———◆———

Q. About 150,000 waterfowl have been observed at one time during fall migration at what wildlife refuge near Havana?

A. Chautauqua National Wildlife Refuge.

———◆———

Q. What Illinois city was the location of the first barbed wire manufacturing company?

A. De Kalb.

———◆———

Q. What announcement did the National Association of Dental Examiners make at their Chicago meeting in August 1918?

A. That they would use no dental instruments or supplies made in Germany.

Q. What Moline-born inventor devised a method to make it practical to have self-starters in automobiles and also founded a company to design and make helicopters?

A. Vincent Bendix.

Q. What city is nicknamed the "forest city" because each block averages more than 100 trees?

A. Rockford.

Q. What 263,363-acre national forest in southern Illinois extends from the Mississippi River to the Ohio?

A. Shawnee.

Q. Mechanical engineer G. W. Gale Ferris, who built the world's largest entertainment device, the Ferris wheel, for the World's Columbian Exposition in Chicago in 1893, was the resident of what Illinois city?

A. Galesburg.

Q. At the James W. Jardine Water Purification Plant in Chicago, how many gallons of water are chemically treated and filtered per minute?

A. More than one million.

Q. At Moline, in 1875, what inventor and manufacturer produced the world's first riding plow?

A. John Deere.

Q. What noted museum of natural history specializes in the wildlife of the Great Lakes region?

A. Chicago Academy of Science.

Q. What percentage of the six-county Chicago metropolitan area consists of public parkland?

A. More than 18 percent.

———◆———

Q. One of the country's oldest commercial bottling companies markets mineral water from what city's famed mineral springs?

A. Peoria.

———◆———

Q. What chemist, born in Hume, shared the 1943 Nobel Prize for his work determining the nature of vitamin K and for the isolation of the female sex hormone?

A. Edward Adelbert Doisy.

———◆———

Q. At Starved Rock State Park each spring, what natural phenomenon occurs at the head of each of its eighteen canyons?

A. Waterfalls form, often reappearing after a heavy rainfall.

———◆———

Q. What Wheaton native helped organize the U.S. Steel Corporation and had a steel-manufacturing city in Indiana named for him?

A. Elbert Henry Gary.

———◆———

Q. When it was founded in 1893, the Field Museum of Natural History was given what name?

A. Columbian Museum of Chicago.

———◆———

Q. What county is the center of large-scale production of gladioli?

A. Kankakee.

Q. The Argyle Antique Gas Engine Show is held each Labor Day weekend at what town?

A. Colchester.

———◆———

Q. After inventing his famous reaper, Cyrus H. McCormick went to Chicago where he set up his own factory to manufacture it, then merged his holdings into what company?

A. International Harvester.

———◆———

Q. How many kinds of fishes live in Lake Michigan and in smaller Illinois lakes and streams?

A. More than 180.

———◆———

Q. The first known game preserve in the country was established in 1868 and stocked with birds and animals by Judge J. D. Canton at what town?

A. Ottawa.

———◆———

Q. Before the pioneers cleared the land, what percentage of Illinois was forested?

A. 40 percent.

———◆———

Q. Today, what percentage of Illinois is forested?

A. 10 percent.

———◆———

Q. What inventor of a system of shorthand founded a school in Chicago to teach his method and other business subjects?

A. John Robert Gregg.

Q. The Shawnee Hills, a region of valleys, woods, river bluffs, and forested hills, have been given what nickname?

A. Illinois Ozarks.

Q. What two counties have large reserves of tripoli, a chalky material used as a polishing powder for metal and glass?

A. Alexander and Union.

Q. What Chicago-based packer was the first to slaughter meat for shipment to the East, an enterprise that became a year-round business with the introduction of the refrigerated railroad car?

A. Gustavus Franklin Swift.

Q. What is the nation's busiest airport?

A. Chicago's O'Hare International Airport.

Q. The Time Museum, featuring an extensive collection of timekeeping devices from around the world, including an atomic clock, may be visited at what city?

A. Rockford.

Q. In 1893-94, what Illinois-born brothers built the first successful gasoline-powered automobile in America?

A. The Duryea brothers: Charles E., born in Canton; and J. Frank, born in Washburn.

Q. What controversial economist was awarded the 1976 Nobel Prize for economics while he was on the faculty of the University of Chicago?

A. Milton Friedman.

Q. What is the nation's oldest agronomic experiment field, under continuous cultivation since 1876?

A. Morrow Plots, at the University of Illinois, Urbana-Champaign.

Q. The state's only quaking bog, exhibiting all stages of aquatic to terrestrial plant succession, is protected at what site?

A. Volo Bog State Natural Area.

Q. At what rate of speed did the Chicago fire burn?

A. Sixty-five acres per hour.

Q. What is the lowest part of the state of Illinois?

A. Alexander County along the Mississippi River, 279 feet above sea level.

Q. The Fragile Kingdom, a study in the ecology of survival and the role of humans in it, is a major component of what zoo in a residential suburb of Chicago?

A. Brookfield Zoo.

Q. The last of a series of navigational and flood control dams that make up the Illinois Waterway may be viewed at what city?

A. Alton.

Q. In 1960, one of the nation's largest electric-power nuclear reactors was completed at what city?

A. Dresden.

Q. Arnold and Mabel Beckman donated how much money to the University of Illinois to found the Beckman Institute for Advanced Science and Technology in the 1980s?

A. $40 million, said to be the largest gift ever given to a public university.

Q. In what year did John James Audubon, famed ornithologist and conservationist, visit the Cache Basin Swamp?

A. 1810.

Q. The Apollo 8 command module that orbited the moon is displayed in what museum?

A. Museum of Science and Industry, Chicago.

Q. What is said to be the largest indoor mammal marine pavilion in the world, housing whales, dolphins, sea otters, harbor seals, and a colony of penguins?

A. The Oceanarium at the John G. Shedd Aquarium in Chicago.

Q. What is the world's oldest steel-skeleton skyscraper?

A. Architects Daniel Burnham's and John Root's Rookery Building, Chicago.

Q. What natural commodity first made Illinois commercially important?

A. Fur, through trading with Indians during the late 1600s.

Q. What vegetable deposits are found in the lake and swamp regions of northeastern Illinois?

A. Peat, the first stage of nature's formation of coal.

Q. What two counties contain deposits of lead and zinc?

A. Hardin and Jo Daviess.

———————◆———————

Q. The refracting telescope at the Yerkes Observatory, the largest of its kind in the world, is how many feet long?

A. Sixty-three, weighing 760 pounds.

———————◆———————

Q. Why do some homes in Chicago erected before the end of the nineteenth century have the front door cut into the second story?

A. When the sewer system was installed, the swampy subsoil precluded burying sewer lines, so streets were raised to cover the pipes, cutting off existing front entrances.

———————◆———————

Q. Approximately how many kinds of wild plants grow in Illinois?

A. 2,400.

———————◆———————

Q. What is the second most important mineral found in Illinois?

A. Fluorspar.

———————◆———————

Q. Where in Chicago can one find a garden for the blind?

A. Next to the Garfield Park Conservatory, the world's largest conservatory under one roof.

———————◆———————

Q. Grass Lake, one of the Chain O'Lakes, is covered in summer with blossoms of what aquatic flower?

A. American lotus.

Q. In the late 1800s, what natural phenomenon destroyed the town of Kaskaskia, the political and social capital of Illinois in its early days?

A. The Mississippi River changed course, wiping it out.

◆

Q. What gathering in Illinois is considered the midwest's largest "star party"?

A. The Chicago Astronomical Society's AstroFest.

◆

Q. Southern Illinois averages how many inches of precipitation a year, including rain, melted snow, and other forms of moisture?

A. Forty inches.

◆

Q. Dedicated in 1930, what was the first planetarium in the Western Hemisphere?

A. Adler Planetarium, Chicago.

◆

Q. What company that ranks among the world's major manufacturers of construction equipment is headquartered in Peoria?

A. Caterpillar.

◆

Q. What is the largest communications company in Illinois?

A. Ameritech, a telecommunications firm.

◆

Q. Illinois is second only to what state in the raising of hogs?

A. Iowa.

Q. Why was Chicago nicknamed the Windy City?

A. Chicagoans bragged so much about the Columbian Exposition of 1893 that the New York newspaper editor Charles A. Dana called it that, with the gusts coming off Lake Michigan only giving popular credence to the title.

———◆———

Q. What is the specialty of Chicago's John Crerar Library?

A. Science.

———◆———

Q. In addition to Big River, Hidden Springs, and Sand Ridge, what is the fourth Illinois state forest?

A. Trail of Tears.

———◆———

Q. Northern Illinois has about how many inches of snow per year?

A. Thirty.

———◆———

Q. The Chicago area is the nation's second-ranking manufacturing region, after what area?

A. Los Angeles.

———◆———

Q. Where is the Yerkes Observatory, the astronomical observatory belonging to the University of Chicago, situated?

A. Seventy-six miles north of Chicago at Williams Bay on Lake Geneva in Wisconsin.

———◆———

Q. What is the leading manufacturing activity in Illinois?

A. Food processing.

Q. What is the largest commodities exchange in the world?

A. Chicago Board of Trade, where traders buy and sell contracts for corn, soybeans, and other commodities.

———◆———

Q. What is the most important mineral resource of Illinois?

A. Bituminous coal.

———◆———

Q. What Rockford native and faculty member at the University of Chicago became one of the world's leading authorities on archaeology, whose excavations included the uncovering of Megiddo (ancient Armageddon)?

A. James Henry Breasted.

———◆———

Q. Founded in 1900 by William E. Sullivan, what Jacksonville company is the largest manufacturer of Ferris wheels?

A. Eli Bridge Company.

———◆———

Q. How many state parks does Illinois have?

A. Seventy-two.

———◆———

Q. What is the most valuable farm product grown in Illinois?

A. Corn.

———◆———

Q. What industries account for 73 percent of the gross state product?

A. Service.

Q. What leading educator and behavioral scientist in 1896 established the campus laboratory schools at nursery, elementary, and high school levels at the University of Chicago?

A. John Dewey.

———◆———

Q. Motorola, a leading producer of electronic communication equipment, is at home in what city?

A. Schaumburg.

———◆———

Q. When did Chicago become an international seaport?

A. In 1959 with the opening of the St. Lawrence Seaway.

———◆———

Q. In its heyday, how many head of livestock did Chicago's famous Union Stock Yards process annually?

A. Eighteen million.

———◆———

Q. In Cook County, how many acres are administered by the Forest Preserve District to provide scenic woodland for recreation and to help reduce air pollution?

A. 60,000.

———◆———

Q. What leading producer of farm machinery is based in Moline?

A. Deere & Company.

———◆———

Q. Manufacturing accounts for what percent of the gross state product?

A. Twenty.

Q. The Vegiform, a plastic mold that fits over growing plants to force them into unusual shapes, is made by what company in Barrington?

A. Robert Marketing, Inc.

———◆———

Q. What prehistoric geological actions produced the gently rolling, fertile plain that covers about 90 percent of Illinois?

A. Glaciers bringing in materials that became soil and leveling the surface.

———◆———

Q. What three of the largest food-processing companies in the nation are headquartered in Chicago?

A. Beatrice, Quaker Oats, and Sara Lee.

———◆———

Q. How many conservation areas does Illinois have?

A. Thirty-nine.

———◆———

Q. During the 1980s, what three counties in the area around Cook County experienced substantial growth in high-tech industries?

A. Lake, Dupage, and Will.

———◆———

Q. What is the second most valuable farm product grown in Illinois?

A. Soybeans.

———◆———

Q. What is the name for a machine that accelerates electrons for nuclear physics experiments, the first of which was built in 1940 at the University of Illinois, Urbana-Champaign?

A. Betatron.

SCIENCE & NATURE

Q. What is the state insect?

A. The Monarch butterfly.

———◆———

Q. With an average wind speed of 10.4 m.p.h., where does Chicago rank with the windiest cities in the United States?

A. Sixteenth (Great Falls, Montana, is first).

———◆———

Q. How long did the Great Fire of Chicago last?

A. Twenty-seven hours (killing 250 people and destroying 17,450 buildings).

———◆———

Q. Why was a capacity audience drawn to the Chicago Coliseum in April, 1910?

A. To hear commodore Robert Peary describe discovering the North Pole.

———◆———

Q. One of the world's major centers dedicated to research in particle physics, what laboratory boasts the world's highest energy particle accelerator, or atom smasher?

A. Fermi National Accelerator laboratory (Fermilab) at Batavia.

———◆———

Q. In what year did Chicago's famous Union Stock Yards close?

A. 1971, a casualty of the development of regional livestock centers.

———◆———

Q. Who won the Westinghouse Science Talent Search in 1990?

A. Chicagoan Matthew Peter Headrick.

Q. In what Illinois city is the H. Douglas Singer Mental Health Development Center?

A. Rockford.

———◆———

Q. In his book, *The Engineers and the Price System*, what one-time University of Chicago economist assigned to scientists and engineers an important position in building a new planned economic society?

A. Thorstein Veblen.

———◆———

Q. Corn grows on what percentage of Illinois farmland?

A. 40 percent.

———◆———

Q. Chicago is the home of what largest retail company in the United States?

A. Sears, Roebuck and Co.

———◆———

Q. Southern Illinois averages about how many inches of snow per year?

A. Ten.

———◆———

Q. What pathologist, at one time on the faculty of the University of Chicago, had a group of disease-producing organisms named for him?

A. Howard Taylor Ricketts (*rickettsiae*).

———◆———

Q. In the 1850s, what Rockford resident invented and produced a combination reaper and mower that revolutionized the agricultural output of the state?

A. John H. Manny.